What people are saying about

Learning from Tomorrow
Using Strategic Foresight to Prepare for the Next Big Disruption

The COVID-19 crisis has accentuated the need for public and private organizations to embrace a futurist mindset in a period of increasing uncertainty and transformational change. *Learning from Tomorrow* clearly explains how strategic foresight can help you forge resilient plans and strategies capable of managing alternative plausible futures ˄st-pandemic world.

Anne Kabagambe, former F ⁓ World Bank Group

Learning from Tomorrow ⅾ tifying strategic foresight and nⳑ people new to foresight and to existing ρ. ˏk is well researched with a tight narrative, and I'll ⳑ ᴐe buying some copies to help spread the importance of foresight in government through my organization.

Bhreigh Gillis, Design Strategist, Workplace Safety and Insurance Board of Ontario

This book provides an accessible entry to the practice of strategic foresight. Key concepts are explained and the book provides examples of how some of the key tools in the foresight toolkit have been applied across the world, both in the wake of the COVID-19 pandemic and prior. The many scenarios surveyed shows how useful foresight is in this period of uncertainty — and how open the future is. The book should inspire readers to explore the practice of strategic foresight further and provides us with many avenues to do so.

Siv Helen Hesjedal, Chief Knowledge and Operations Officer, Eastern Cape Socio-Economic Consultative Council (South Africa)

Science tells us that anthropogenic threats to the environment and biodiversity are increasing and have serious – and in some cases irreversible — implications for the wellbeing of people, nature and the planet. Strategic foresight can help us assess how trends are evolving, enabling us to take action now to prepare for a wide range of future scenarios. *Learning from Tomorrow* strengthens our capacity to plan wisely and effectively. Every environmental leader should make this a "must read" for 2021.

Scott Edwards, Executive Director, Conservation Strategy Fund

Navigating the complexity of social transformation under emerging threats such as climate change is challenging for today's governments and systems. *Learning from Tomorrow* offers a timely and highly relevant contribution to foresight and anticipatory governance by demonstrating how foresight facilitates robust, long-term planning in the midst of uncertainty. This is certainly a book that will change the way you think tomorrow, and unlock a new thinking of today.

Dr. Rathana Peou Norbert-Munns, Scenarios Coordinator, CGIAR Research Program on Climate Change, Agriculture and Food Security

Even though foresight has become a modern buzzword, it is veiled in mystery to many. Bart Édes fills this concept with life and convincingly shows why it should become an essential element of policy work and in other contexts. *Learning from Tomorrow* is essential reading for everyone who is interested in foresight and, even more, in its practical application.

Marek Prityi, Chief State Advisor, Ministry of Environment, Slovak Republic

RESETTING OUR FUTURE

Learning from Tomorrow

Using Strategic Foresight to Prepare for the Next Big Disruption

Resetting Our Future

Learning from Tomorrow

Using Strategic Foresight to Prepare for
the Next Big Disruption

Bart W. Édes

CHANGEMAKERS
BOOKS

Winchester, UK
Washington, USA

JOHN HUNT PUBLISHING

First published by Changemakers Books, 2021
Changemakers Books is an imprint of John Hunt Publishing Ltd., No. 3 East Street,
Alresford, Hampshire SO24 9EE, UK
office@jhpbooks.com
www.johnhuntpublishing.com
www.changemakers-books.com

For distributor details and how to order please visit the 'Ordering' section on our website.

Text copyright: Bart W. Édes 2020

ISBN: 978 1 78904 763 9
978 1 78904 764 6 (ebook)
Library of Congress Control Number: 2021930487

A CIP catalogue record for this book is available from the British Library.

Design: Stuart Davies

UK: Printed and bound by CPI Group (UK) Ltd, Croydon, CR0 4YY
Printed in North America by CPI GPS partners

We operate a distinctive and ethical publishing philosophy in
all areas of our business, from our global network of authors to
production and worldwide distribution.

Contents

The *Resetting Our Future* Series

At this critical moment of history, with a pandemic raging, we have the rare opportunity for a Great Reset – to choose a different future. This series provides a platform for pragmatic thought leaders to share their vision for change based on their deep expertise. For communities and nations struggling to cope with the crisis, these books will provide a burst of hope and energy to help us take the first difficult steps towards a better future.
– Tim Ward, publisher, Changemakers Books

What if Solving the Climate Crisis Is Simple?
Tom Bowman, President of Bowman Change, Inc., and writing-team lead for the U.S. ACE National Strategic Planning Framework

Zero Waste Living, the 80/20 Way
The Busy Person's Guide to a Lighter Footprint
Stephanie Miller, Founder of Zero Waste in DC, and former Director, IFC Climate Business Department

A Chicken Can't Lay a Duck Egg
How COVID-19 Can Solve the Climate Crisis
Graeme Maxton, (former Secretary-General of the Club of Rome), and Bernice Maxton-Lee (former Director, Jane Goodall Institute)

A Global Playbook for the Next Pandemic
Anne Kabagambe, former World Bank Executive Director

Power Switch
How We Can Reverse Extreme Inequality
Paul O'Brien, VP Policy and Advocacy, Oxfam America

Impact ED
How Community College Entrepreneurship Creates Equity and Prosperity
Rebecca Corbin (President & CEO, National Association of Community College Entrepreneurship), Andrew Gold and Mary Beth Kerly (both business faculty, Hillsborough Community College)

Empowering Public Climate Action in the United States
Tom Bowman (President of Bowman Change, Inc.) and Deb Morrison (Learning Scientist, University of Washington)

Learning from Tomorrow
Using Strategic Foresight to Prepare for the Next Big Disruption
Bart Édes, former North American Representative, Asian Development Bank

Provocateurs Not Philanthropists
Turning Good Intentions into Global Impact
Maiden R. Manzanal-Frank, Strategy Maven at GlobalStakes Consulting

SMART Futures for a Flourishing World
A Paradigm Shift for Achieving the Sustainable Development Goals
Dr. Claire Nelson, Chief Visionary Officer and Lead Futurist, The Futures Forum

Cut Super Climate Pollutants, Now!
The Ozone Treaty's Urgent Lessons for Speeding Up Climate Action
Alan Miller (former World Bank representative for global climate negotiations) and Durwood Zaelke, (President, The Institute for Governance & Sustainable Development, and co-director, The Program on Governance for Sustainable Development at UC Santa Barbara)

Lead Different

Designing a Post-COVID Paradigm for Thriving at Work and at Home

Monica Brand, Lisa Neuberger & Wendy Teleki

Reconstructing Blackness

Rev. Charles Howard, Chaplin, University of Pennsylvania, Philadelphia

www.ResettingOurFuture.com

Foreword

by Thomas Lovejoy

The pandemic has changed our world. Lives have been lost. Livelihoods as well. Far too many face urgent problems of health and economic security, but almost all of us are reinventing our lives in one way or another. Meeting the immediate needs of the less fortunate is obviously a priority, and a big one. But beyond those compassionate imperatives, there is also tremendous opportunity for what some people are calling a "Great Reset." This series of books, Resetting Our Future, is designed to provide pragmatic visionary ideas and stimulate a fundamental rethink of the future of humanity, nature and the economy.

I find myself thinking about my parents, who had lived through the Second World War and the Great Depression, and am still impressed by the sense of frugality they had attained. When packages arrived in the mail, my father would save the paper and string; he did it so systematically I don't recall our ever having to buy string. Our diets were more careful: whether it could be afforded or not, beef was restricted to once a week. When aluminum foil—the great boon to the kitchen—appeared, we used and washed it repeatedly until it fell apart. Bottles, whether Coca-Cola or milk, were recycled.

Waste was consciously avoided. My childhood task was to put out the trash; what goes out of my backdoor today is an unnecessary multiple of that. At least some of it now goes to recycling but a lot more should surely be possible.

There was also a widespread sense of service to a larger community. Military service was required of all. But there was also the Civilian Conservation Corps, which had provided jobs and repaired the ecological destruction that had generated the Dust Bowl. The Kennedy administration introduced the Peace

Corps and the President's phrase "Ask not what your country can do for you but what you can do for your country" still resonates in our minds.

There had been antecedents, but in the 1970s there was a global awakening about a growing environmental crisis. In 1972, The United Nations held its first conference on the environment at Stockholm. Most of the modern US institutions and laws about environment were established under moderate Republican administrations (Nixon and Ford). Environment was seen not just as appealing to "greenies" but also as a thoughtful conservative's issue. The largest meeting of Heads of State in history, the Earth Summit, took place in Rio de Janeiro in 1992 and three international conventions—climate change, biodiversity (on which I was consulted) and desertification—came into existence.

But three things changed. First, there now are three times as many people alive today as when I was born and each new person deserves a minimum quality of life. Second, the sense of frugality was succeeded by a growing appetite for affluence and an overall attitude of entitlement. And third, conservative political advisors found advantage in demonizing the environment as comity vanished from the political dialogue.

Insufficient progress has brought humanity and the environment to a crisis state. The CO_2 level in the atmosphere at 415 ppm (parts per million) is way beyond a non-disruptive level around 350 ppm. (The pre-industrial level was 280 ppm.)

Human impacts on nature and biodiversity are not just confined to climate change. Those impacts will not produce just a long slide of continuous degradation. The pandemic is a direct result of intrusion upon, and destruction of, nature as well as wild-animal trade and markets. The scientific body of the UN Convention on Biological Diversity warned in 2020 that we could lose a million species unless there are major changes in human interactions with nature.

We still can turn those situations around. Ecosystem restoration at scale could pull carbon back out of the atmosphere for a soft landing at 1.5 degrees of warming (at 350 ppm), hand in hand with a rapid halt in production and use of fossil fuels. The Amazon tipping point where its hydrological cycle would fail to provide enough rain to maintain the forest in southern and eastern Amazonia can be solved with major reforestation. The oceans' biology is struggling with increasing acidity, warming and ubiquitous pollution with plastics: addressing climate change can lower the first two and efforts to remove plastics from our waste stream can improve the latter.

Indisputably, we need a major reset in our economies, what we produce, and what we consume. We exist on an amazing living planet, with a biological profusion that can provide humanity a cornucopia of benefits—and more that science has yet to reveal—and all of it is automatically recyclable because nature is very good at that. Scientists have determined that we can, in fact, feed all the people on the planet, and the couple billion more who may come, by a combination of selective improvements of productivity, eliminating food waste and altering our diets (which our doctors have been advising us to do anyway).

The Resetting Our Future series is intended to help people think about various ways of economic and social rebuilding that will support humanity for the long term. There is no single way to do this and there is plenty of room for creativity in the process, but nature with its capacity for recovery and for recycling can provide us with much inspiration, including ways beyond our current ability to imagine.

Ecosystems do recover from shocks, but the bigger the shock, the more complicated recovery can be. At the end of the Cretaceous period (66 million years ago) a gigantic meteor slammed into the Caribbean near the Yucatan and threw up so much dust and debris into the atmosphere that much of biodiversity perished. It was *sayonara* for the dinosaurs; their only surviving close relatives were precursors to modern day birds. It certainly was not a good time for life on Earth.

The clear lesson of the pandemic is that it makes no sense to generate a global crisis and then hope for a miracle. We are lucky to have the pandemic help us reset our relation to the Living Planet as a whole. We already have building blocks like the United Nations Sustainable Development Goals and various environmental conventions to help us think through more effective goals and targets. The imperative is to rebuild with humility and imagination, while always conscious of the health of the living planet on which we have the joy and privilege to exist.

Dr. Thomas E. Lovejoy is Professor of Environmental Science and Policy at George Mason University and a Senior Fellow at the United Nations Foundation. A world-renowned conservation biologist, Dr. Lovejoy introduced the term "biological diversity" to the scientific community.

Acknowledgements

This book embraces the view that Strategic Foresight aids government organizations in making better decisions and improving service to the citizenry. A highlight of my career to date was collaborating with Bob Bonwitt, who spent much of his professional life working to advance democracy, rule of law and human rights, particularly in countries of the former Eastern Bloc as they emerged from totalitarian rule. Bob, who died in July 2018, was a modest, intelligent, honorable and visionary man who inspired those working with him. He was a dedicated public servant of the highest order and did his part to create a more peaceful world with better governance.

While I have done plenty of writing over the years, it has never been in the form of a complete book, even a short one. This marks my first attempt. I would not have undertaken this effort without the steadfast encouragement and experienced counsel of Tim Ward, whose ability to multitask among a range of meaningful projects continues to boggle the mind. He never ceases to seed the world with ideas and tools to promote civility, social justice, sustainability and effective communications. Thank you, Tim, for giving me the push, and for your extraordinary patience.

For more than twenty years, Joanne Weston has encouraged me to pursue my dreams and goals. She is always there for me, and has always believed in me. Joanne is not only a highly talented and caring professional coach, but also a fearsome tennis player, nurturing mother, and my reliable, fun partner in life.

Introduction

The coronavirus disease (COVID-19), and the government measures taken to control it, has severely disrupted our lives. As of this writing, the crisis has killed more than 2 million people, precipitated the greatest economic downturn since the Great Depression, caused widespread unemployment, derailed progress toward the Sustainable Development Goals, and left scars that will take many years to heal.

Governments found themselves unprepared for pandemic, although it could hardly be considered a surprise that one would be coming sooner rather than later. Epidemiologists warned us time and time again that another global pandemic was on its way. They did not have to dig deep into the past for examples, as there have been plenty within the last three decades.

In 1994, science writer Laure Garrett highlighted the risk of dangerous emerging diseases in the bestseller *The Coming Plague*. Just three years later, the highly pathogenic influenza A virus subtype H5N1 struck fear into the hearts of Hong Kong residents, and then emerged in multiple countries in the first decade of this century. SARS killed hundreds in Southeast Asia and Canada in 2002 and 2003.

The wicked Ebola hemorrhagic fever felled thousands in West Africa between 2013 and 2016, and has returned every year since to cause more pain and death. In short, we should have seen COVID-19 coming, and properly prepared for a scenario like the one that unfolded in 2020. Indeed, after the Ebola crisis, Bill Gates delivered a TedX presentation in which he called for scenario planning and other steps to prepare for the inevitable next pandemic.

In a report on early lessons learned from the current pandemic, the reputed Council on Foreign Relations observed that, "the US government, foreign counterparts, and international agencies commissioned multiple scenarios and tabletop exercises that anticipated with uncanny accuracy the trajectory that a major outbreak could take, the complex national and global challenges it would create, and the glaring gaps and limitations in national and international capacity it would reveal."[1]

There are of course risks other than health-related ones that should have our attention. Such risks will, of course, vary in significance depending on the country, community, and organization concerned. The inevitability of different kinds of disruptions makes it important to pay closer attention to signs that changes are afoot.

Scholars Ann Florini and Sunil Sharma argue that, "despite the unpredictability of complex systems, such techniques as horizon scanning and scenario analysis can often detect signs of emerging problems that could cause systemic disruption."[2] These techniques, or methods, are among the ways in which Strategic Foresight (or for purposes of this book, simply Foresight) is carried out.

In this book's first chapter, I will aim to demystify Foresight and explain how it can help organizations better prepare for the future. One of the important international forums for sharing experience and insights in this field is the Government Foresight Community, convened annually since 2014 by the Organization for Economic Cooperation and Development (OECD). Established in 1961, the OECD is a forum of democratic nations with market economies. The 37 (mostly European) member countries compare public policies, explore solutions to major challenges across economic themes and sectors, identify good practices, and coordinate policies.

The Government Foresight Community is one of many thematic networks through which representatives of OECD member countries interact and learn from each other. At the community's most recent in-person meeting (before the pandemic), government participants – all responsible for

Foresight functions in their countries – identified obstacles to exploring plausible futures in order to improve policies and achieve well-being. The major obstacles they identified were lack of awareness about the need for Foresight, and lack of access to user-friendly Foresight products, tools, guides, and training.[3]

I wrote this book to help overcome these obstacles. I want planners and decision-makers in organizations to see Foresight as a practical tool to support thinking about the medium-to-long term, and make more informed policy choices. Having spent 30 years in public sector organizations, I have repeatedly observed missed opportunities to improve how an organization performs and prepares for the days ahead by thoughtfully "factoring in the future."

The target audiences of this book are those who play a role in planning, policy and strategy development, resource allocation, and rulemaking. Although most of the examples provided in this book come from public sector bodies, the insights and tools described can equally benefit organizations in the not-for-profit and private sectors.

One of the organizations that has become renowned for developing future scenarios – a key method in the practice of Foresight – is Royal Dutch Shell PLC, a global multinational enterprise. In 1965, the petroleum giant launched a long-term studies program, and began preparing oil-price scenarios six years later. Its scenarios work helped to prepare the corporation for production constraints imposed by oil-rich countries. Over the years, Shell has shared big picture global scenarios on its corporate website.[4] I encourage you to take a look.

Notwithstanding the examples provided by Shell and several other large companies, particularly in the high-tech sector, only about one-quarter of Fortune 500 firms practice Foresight in some capacity in-house.[5]

An increasing number of academic institutions are offering

courses and academic credentials in Foresight, such as the University of Houston, which offers a professional certificate and master of science degree in Foresight. Even primary and secondary school students in public schools in Jackson, Mississippi, can learn some basics about Foresight and futurism at a free after-school program offered by a local foundation.

Foresight "travels" well. Given its affordability, flexibility, and range of methods, it can be used in vastly different cultural and geographic contexts. While it is true that Foresight exercises can be both time- and resource-intensive, you and your organization can begin to practice Foresight without great cost once you have learned the basics. The investment can end up saving your organization trouble and costs by revealing future risks and opportunities.

For example, in 2020, a team of professors at the Brasilia campus of Brazil's Mackenzie Presbyterian University quickly assembled 390 experts to develop four post-COVID-19 scenarios[6] for the economic and social impacts in Brazil through the year 2022. Due to the volunteer contributions of many experts, the rapid scenario-development process required minimal budget. The outputs were used by several government departments in formulating short-term strategies.

Florini and Sharma describe the current global situation as follows: "Driven by increasing fragility in our political, social, economic, and financial orders—all dependent on a natural environment nearing the brink—these apparent bolts from the blue will keep striking. With all systems simultaneously in flux, the 21st century is set to experience massive disruptions that pose serious and possibly existential threats to society."[7]

If they are right, then we have reason to be anxious. Yet we are not helpless, as we have tools at our disposal to build strength and muster courage in the face of tumultuous events. By identifying drivers of change, and systematically formulating plausible scenarios that could emerge from their interactions, we empower ourselves to prepare, and to act with confidence. This is the reason why any organization can benefit from the use of Foresight.

Chapter 1

What Is Foresight and What Does it Do?

The future often surprises us. Looking back at recent history – what used to be the future – reveals unexpected developments. We marvel, "how on earth did we get here?" For example, take Facebook, which was launched in 2004. Who among the Baby Boomers and Gen Xers who were teens or adults at the time thought that Facebook would become a massively influential social media innovation with more than 2.5 billion users? And who, in 2010, imagined that gay marriage would, within just a few years, be legalized in dozens of countries? And what about Donald Trump's victory in the United States (US) presidential election in 2016? His successful campaign that year was seen as unlikely as late as the morning of Election Day by most expert political analysts and seasoned pollsters.

Although we cannot know with certainty what the next decade or two will bring, the future is not like a hermetically sealed black box. While many of us did not foresee the rise of Facebook, the growing acceptance of gay marriage, or the election of Donald Trump, Foresight exercises carried out early in this century generated scenarios that included disruptive technological, social and political changes of the sort that gave rise to these events and trends. In short, the future is not a complete mystery.

The OECD defines Foresight as a structured and systematic way of using ideas about the future to anticipate and better prepare for change. It is about exploring different plausible futures that could arise, and the opportunities and challenges they could present. We then use those ideas to make better decisions and to take action.[1]

Foresight brings together insights from different fields – economics, systems theory, engineering, sociology, and others. It explores a range of plausible alternative futures by identifying drivers that influence what could come next. Foresight investigates change from a systems perspective that recognizes that a system consists of parts, and that those parts and the overall system, interact with each other. Foresight examines how the interactions take place and what they generate.

It is important to understand that Foresight does not give us the power to predict the future or perceive all that could happen. It is not the same as forecasting, which is mainly based on linear extrapolation from historical data, evidence and probability. While forecasting draws on what we have learned from the past, Foresight adopts a nonlinear, forward-looking view of change. It illuminates directions and possibilities, giving us a chance to consider options. In a sense, Foresight helps us learn from the future (or, more precisely, alternative plausible futures).

When confronted by uncertainty, Foresight provides a structured way to anticipate and analyze possible trends. In doing so, it can bring a certain steadiness to decision-making systems tested by turbulent events and transformational changes to the economy and society.

Foresight has become an increasingly established field of practice with a professional cadre of experts aiding organizations seeking to benefit from it. Foresight is being used to improve understanding of demographic change, consumer values, impacts of climate change, scientific and technological discoveries, military strategies, employment generation, and key sectors of the economy – education, energy, finance, health, housing, transport, tourism, and others.

A competent government Foresight system is effective at collecting, analyzing and interpreting pertinent data and information; identifying how different drivers of change interact with each other and create more changes; elaborating alternative scenarios based on what has been learned; developing plans and strategies that take into account the scenarios; and then undertaking effective implementation, monitoring and evaluation.

It is not easy to put all this together, as it requires changes in the behavior of people and organizations. Foresight challenges its users to think differently and be open to new ways of interpreting the future.

As time passes, and decisions are made and events take place, *possible futures* emerge. These are based on knowledge we don't have today but may acquire one day. A subset of these possible futures comprises those that could happen – *plausible futures*. These describe what could happen based on what we know of the world today. Futures that are likely to occur if we remain on the current trajectory are *probable*. *Preferable* futures are those which we would like to see emerge in the period ahead.

The Futures Cone (below) offers a visual way of understanding these different types of futures. One needs to explore the changes that are taking place and what is driving

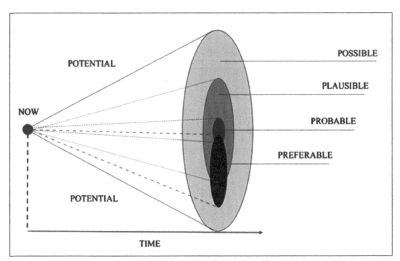

Adapted from: Peter Voros, https://thevoroscope.com/2017/02/24/the-futures-cone-use-and-history/

them to understand what may be possible futures. Many trends are visible and well known, and influence policy decisions that have been made. However, emerging trends are not adequately recognized and understood to contribute to decision-making. Some versions of the Futures Cone include another category on the edge above the possible – *preposterous futures* ("these could never come to pass!"). Given the accelerated change and heightened uncertainty that characterize our times, the lines between plausible, possible, probable and, yes, preposterous futures have become somewhat blurred.

Foresight in a turbulent world

In October 2019, the Johns Hopkins Center for Health Security, Nuclear Threat Initiative, and Economist Intelligence Unit, jointly published the Global Health Security Index comparing 195 countries on their global health security preparedness. The US was ranked as the most prepared country in the world to respond to an epidemic or pandemic. And yet, just months later, the US failed miserably to capitalize on its purported ability to prevent, detect and respond to a health emergency.[2]

The myriad reasons for this sad state of affairs in the US included an initially delayed and then poorly coordinated official response; inconsistent messaging from leaders; widespread public reluctance to following sensible guidelines (wearing facemasks, social distancing); a highly-charged partisan political environment during the high-stakes election year of 2020; and inadequate funding for public health.

The pandemic, and economic recession and jobs crisis it precipitated, shook a world already undergoing great transformation in the form of climate change, digital and biological convergence, growing populism, automation, advances in artificial intelligence, adoption of blockchain and crypto currencies, resource depletion and biodiversity loss, weakening of the rules-based global trading system, shifting consumer behavior, record numbers of refugees, withdrawal of the US from its global leadership role, and the continued rise of Asia, as well as an intensifying US-China rivalry. We are truly living in a time of volatility, uncertainty, complexity and ambiguity – or, as commonly referred to by Foresight experts, "VUCO."

Added to this intermingling of powerful currents has been the dramatic reawakening of a racial justice movement in the US – a movement that quickly took on international dimensions with millions protesting worldwide. In addition, western US states (and Australian ones) have been experiencing terrifying wildfires – harbingers of what more advanced stages of climate change hold in store for humanity.

These disruptions have added to the complexity and uncertainty of modern life. Now, more than ever, responsible public governance requires better preparation for the future. This is where Foresight comes in. Foresight improves governance by providing a structured way of exploring different plausible futures, and the challenges and possibilities they could present. Foresight introduces new considerations into policy deliberations that current policies and institutions have not previously taken into account.

Commenting on this youthful decade's greatest crisis, Steve Sanford, director of the Center for Strategic Foresight at the US General Accounting Office, stated that, "the risks and impacts of a pandemic were not unknown. I'm a big proponent of Foresight work, and I think it's important to do, but just as important is translating that work into action. I think that's one of the major lessons that has come out of the pandemic."[3]

Peter Jones, a Toronto-based expert on social and design research, notes that, "Foresight provides a necessary competency for defining and investing in the right direction of future policy and action, by articulating future problematics with multiple foresight methods. While social and technological futures cannot be precisely predicted, future scenarios and prospectuses can be designed to inform options and trajectories for intervention and new policy."[4] Foresight is not suited to every decision-making situation. If the context is simple and clear, and the time frame short – say next month, or within the next couple of years – applying Foresight to a policy question or concern may be overkill. But where great uncertainty and complexity are present, and the time frame concerned stretches into the medium-to-long term, Foresight methodologies can be highly useful. Here are ten benefits that Foresight brings to organizations that use it:

Promotes innovation

Foresight nudges organizations into thinking more broadly about possibilities, including fresh ideas, approaches, products and services. In the process, it stimulates innovation to address challenges that emerge from alternative future scenarios.

Enhances agility

Foresight leads organizations to anticipate deviations from today's norms and trends. With Foresight, organizations begin to think differently about how to achieve their goals, the various paths for achieving those goals, and the diversions and obstacles that may appear along the way. Organizations using Foresight are more agile and better situated to adapt quickly to changes.

Tests critical assumptions

Policy is always based on assumptions, some implicit, some explicit. Foresight challenges assumptions and can uncover invalid or otherwise flawed assumptions that form the foundation for important decisions and plans.

Enhances Resilience

An organization that uses Foresight strengthens its capacity to bounce back quickly from difficulties. It also draws attention to possibilities of a low-probability, high-impact event that might mark a change in direction for a trend or system (a black swan event).

Improves competitiveness

Foresight strengthens an organization's ability to compete effectively with peers and rivals that have failed to consider and prepare for multiple future scenarios. Foresight can assist organizations in coming up with more innovative offerings for their customers and clients, and anticipating their evolving desires.

Boosts employee satisfaction

Foresight draws on expertise and views within the organization, recognizing the value in its personnel. Employees respond positively to the opportunity to construct a common vision and to contribute to their organization's future.

Promotes learning

The inquisitive and exploratory nature of Foresight directly contributes to learning lessons and developing new insights through the engagement of different disciplines and specialties. Some governments and companies make the findings of their Foresight studies freely available as a contribution to knowledge sharing.

Facilitates public participation

Foresight involves the sort of research that one can do at their computer, but it also requires engagement with others, in and ideally outside the organization. It provides an opportunity to involve a diversity of stakeholders in developing shared visions of what could come to pass. In doing so, Foresight can nurture community and societal ownership, as well as a collective sense of shared interest and forward-looking purpose.

Improves planning and strategizing

Foresight expands and reframes the range of alternative futures beyond the most expected ones. It gives organizations more information and insight with which to plan for the years ahead. It also generates options for experimentation with innovative approaches, and allows stress testing of possible strategies and policies.

Empowers people and organizations

Through Foresight, organizations embrace uncertainty, rather than attempt the impossibility of trying to control it. Foresight enhances an organization's confidence, and strength. Fear of the unknown fades as plausible alternative futures come into view.

What stops organizations from using Foresight?

Given Foresight's value proposition, what stops public sector organizations from using it? One leading reason is the immediate focus on the present. While an increasing number of governments use Foresight methods, the imperative to respond to the needs of the "here and now" draws decision-makers away from a look further down the road. Political leaders and partisan appointees in government ministries/departments often employ short-term thinking, connected to upcoming votes or elections. Their more immediate priorities become the priorities of the public servants who report to them.

Although Foresight has gained a stronger foothold over time, it still remains a mystery to many. The terminology and techniques require some thought and practice to understand. Foresight is sometimes seen as abstract, theoretical, or lofty and removed from hard-nosed reality in a competitive world.

Since technology is a key influencer of many major changes that lie ahead, Foresight scenarios can appear lifted from the script of a sci-fi movie. It can be a little difficult to explain Foresight, thus leading to misinterpretations that it is some sort of guessing game or drawn-out brainstorming session. Because Foresight challenges current assumptions and is not bound to statistics on earlier developments, skeptics may allege that it is poorly grounded in reality as we perceive it today.

Busy leaders focused on several competing demands may not be convinced by the value of contemplating widely divergent scenarios of the future. They have enough on their plate without having to sort through possibilities that each demand a different approach in planning. Decision-makers prefer certainty and clarity – things that Foresight does not promise.

In short, it is a big step for an organization to cross the threshold into the world of Foresight. An investment of budgetary and staffing resources is required (to monitor signals of change, perform research, solicit expert opinions, hold workshops, and engage professional outside expertise). Even if modest relative to the organization's capacity, the investment inevitably is weighed against alternatives that are better known and have a track record within the organization. It can be hard for decision-makers to justify the use of precious budgetary resources to plan for distant futures when clients, citizens and stakeholders have needs that must be met this week.

There is also the fear factor. The future can be intimidating, and some long-term futures portray a world that is, frankly speaking, somewhat dystopian. For a Foresight exercise to be truly credible, it needs to consider possibilities that we may be afraid to discuss, or which are politically sensitive or socially controversial. We don't want to think about bad things happening. But the freedom to explore what could happen in the period ahead is essential to formulating plausible alternative futures. Without such freedom, the process becomes less useful.

Public sector organizations are not known for their nimbleness and agility, and their employees lack incentives to innovate and propose fundamental changes – the kind of changes that Foresight often reveals as both prudent and sensible. Career civil servants aren't rewarded for rocking the boat in a hierarchical structure. The use of Foresight becomes more promising when the organization using it is creative and open to new ways of working.

If an organization has courageously forged ahead, deliberated even unpleasant possibilities, and completed a well-designed Foresight exercise, it may find something unexpected and potentially threatening. The scenarios resulting from the exercise may imply unpalatable decisions and actions. This can create great unease, and the temptation may arise to put the "interesting study" aside.

As you see, there are some obstacles to overcome. So, why persevere? Refer back to the ten benefits previously cited. They are real, as more and more organizations are discovering, and not only government organizations. Many of us have work-related responsibilities to provide sound counsel in areas under our purview. We are doing an incomplete job if we are not presenting alternative perspectives.

The proverbial scale is tilting in the direction of "more Foresight" in organizations. COVID-19 has spilled out on to a terrain already experiencing tremors of great change, and it is breaking down resistance to investing in study of the future. The pandemic has highlighted the risk of not anticipating and preparing adequately for significant risks. "Future proofing" our policies just seems to make good sense.

Chapter 2

Putting Foresight to Work in Your Organization

Foresight encompasses a variety of methodologies. Many were developed in the US, including at the California-based RAND Corporation, a not-for-profit institution that helps improve policy and decision-making through research analysis. RAND was an early leader in creating structured ways of thinking about the future, starting not long after the end of World War II.[1]

In 1964, RAND published a fascinating report based on an experimental trend-predicting exercise extending decades into the future. The report used the Delphi Technique (described below) to solicit opinions of experts in six areas: scientific breakthroughs, population growth, automation, space progress, probability and prevention of war, and future weapon systems.

Governments in many high-income countries have used Foresight for decades to study questions of enormous significance, like the potential for armed conflict among nations. But Foresight is also useful in gaining insights into more localized concerns, such as traffic patterns, water needs, and school enrolment. Different organizations apply Foresight in different ways. The approach taken will depend in part on the time and resources available, as well as the complexity of the issue considered.

The Foresight process entails analyzing a situation to assess what seems to be happening. Initial analysis aims to ascertain whether what *seems* to be happening really *is* what is occurring. The process then moves to considering what might occur in the future. At this juncture, organizations can then deliberate what actions might be required, and what they actually will do based on the insights generated.

Steps for conducting Foresight

There are multiple ways to use Foresight in an organization. The six steps outlined below are common to many Foresight exercises and should be viewed as illustrative. Methods are flexibly adapted to different contexts, depending on factors such as the strategic question being explored, the available time for study and deliberation, human and budgetary resources, and the expertise at hand. To go more in depth on Foresight methodologies and processes, check out the resources (all free!) in the "Where to learn more" section of Chapter 5.

The following steps are, in order: 1) identify the issue; 2) clarify assumptions; 3) scan the horizon; 4) map systems and explore drivers of change; 5) prepare scenarios; and 6) develop policy options.

1. Identify the issue

Applying Foresight begins with framing the issue (or problem) which is characterized by uncertainty. For example, it could be something like "What will the global renewable energy market look like in 2027?" Or perhaps, "How will higher education be delivered in 2030?" Another possibility is, "How will urban transit systems operate in 2035?" Looking further ahead, one might want to know, "What will be the state of the oceans in 2050?"

As you will notice, all of these hypothetical examples include a year somewhere off in the distance. While not all Foresight studies aim to describe scenarios up to a particular year, many do, since a specific time period provides an anchor and context for the exercise, thus helping to focus the minds of participants. Foresight tends to be used for assessing plausible alternative futures a decade, or several decades, from today. (For a period of a few months or just a couple of years, you are probably better off using forecasting techniques.)

2. Clarify assumptions

One great use of Foresight is for testing assumptions. Every plan or policy is based on assumptions, whether those assumptions are stated or not (often not). Once the issue for study is identified, you can examine the underlying assumptions. This can be uncomfortable, because we usually don't spell out all of the important assumptions that underpin our plans. But this is an essential step in performing a rigorous Foresight process.

Faulty logic or factual errors in one's assumptions can lead to poor policies and outcomes. Assumptions can be revealed by sharing ideas within the organization, and by observing those that exist externally in the public realm. They should be stated explicitly and challenged for their validity and relevance. One possibility is that it may become clear that an assumption might not be true. In such instances, further research is required if that assumption is an important underpinning of your organization's operations and policies.

Casual Layered Analysis is a futures research method pioneered by influential futurist Sohail Inayatullah. It is a means for digging into the underlying causes and worldviews that contribute to a problem or situation. The analysis is carried out by a group of participants (holding different views) on four levels of causality: litany, social or systemic causes, discourse/worldview, and myth/metaphor, with litany at the top. It can be useful for challenging assumptions and reframing issues.

The first two levels are more visible than the deeper third and fourth levels. Litany identifies current issues, assumptions, facts and data. It is where the participants identify the problem based on current understanding of reality. On the next layer down, the social or systemic causes underlying the litany are studied. Here participants investigate what has caused the problem.

Dominant worldviews and mindsets are examined on the third level, where participants explore the values, culture, and mental models that support the litany. On the fourth and deepest layer, participants consider the foundational myths, metaphors and archetypes that influence the unconscious and emotional undertones beneath the issues. Discussion at this layer evokes emotional responses to the issue being explored.

After having proceeded through the four layers, participants can return to the fourth layer to select a different myth or narrative to formulate a new and alternative future scenario, moving back up through the layers. From this scenario, new possibilities can be drawn out and then applied to solutions, policies, and other types of actions for implementation. The results of a Casual Layered Analysis exercise are often presented as an "iceberg," as shown below.

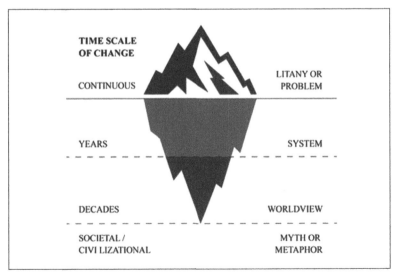

Adapted from version by Inayatullah, S., D. List, and A. Hines at libarynth.org.

Ultimately, Casual Layered Analysis draws on multiple perspectives to help identify driving forces and worldviews shaping an issue. It supports a critical examination of conventional thinking and helps to generate a shared view of possible future outcomes that mark a departure from prevailing paradigms. Community design strategist Ilana Lipsett provides an excellent example of applying Casual Layered Analysis to complex contemporary social challenges by exploring both racial injustice and climate change. You can find it here: https://www.iftf.org/future-now/article-detail/using-causal-layered-analysis-for-transformational-change/.

3. Scan the horizon

A foundational Foresight methodology is the horizon (or environment) scan, which seeks to detect early indications of change, including weak signals, and their potential future impacts. Weak signals are indications of an emerging issue that could become significant. They are bits of information that can help an organization become aware of changes taking place, or which could soon take place. Weak signals may be noticed during an analysis of operational data, or be something new in social media.

Horizon scanning is something that organizations can (and should) do on a regular basis, not only as part of a structured Foresight process on a certain topic. When a major transformation is emerging, there will be signals of the change (such as the adoption of cashless transactions or the democratization of space travel). Being attuned to such signals can enable you to better grasp possible futures.

Horizon scanning is conducted through desk research, focus groups, and expert surveys. A variety of techniques can be used at this stage, including the Delphi Method, which is used to seek opinions from experts on a topic(s) relevant to a particular Foresight exercise. It involves rounds of surveying a group of experts. After each round, the experts' replies are aggregated and then shared with the experts, who are given the opportunity to amend their answers in light of the aggregated group response. Different Foresight studies apply variations of this approach.

For example, in 2018, close to 30 experts in futures research and horizon scanning, advisors to policy makers, researchers, and practitioners of conservation and other aspects of environmental science conducted a horizon scan of emerging issues that were likely to be relevant to global conservation in the following year.[2]

Participants' expertise covered diverse conservation-related disciplines, including marine, freshwater, and terrestrial ecology; agriculture and land use; microbiology; conservation practice and technology; sustainability; environmental management; policy; economics; research programming; science communication; and professional horizon scanning. The participants were affiliated with academia, government, and nongovernment organizations.

The scan was being carried out for the tenth consecutive year. The process and findings were subsequently reported in a paper written by Bill Sutherland of Cambridge University's Department of Zoology, and his collaborators. Using a modified version of the Delphi Method, participants identified 15 topics that could have major impacts on society's ability to conserve regional or global biodiversity, but for which the conservation community currently has generally low awareness.

The process began with participants consulting their professional networks one-on-one, via wider conversations and requests at meetings, and through targeted social media and group email requests. Nearly 500 persons were consulted, leading to the collection of 91 issues.

The criteria used for considering the suitability of topics

for consideration in the exercise were: novelty (or, for better-known issues, a marked change in the intensity or nature of their impact); the potential for major positive or negative effects on the conservation of global or regional biological diversity in the future; and a reasonable likelihood that the importance of the topic would increase.

The 91 collected issues were given to each participant, who scored each one from 0 to 1000 on the basis of both its novelty and the potential magnitude of its effects. The experts were provided the option of adding comments on each topic related to the criteria. Typical comments from participants included issues already being too well known, issues being similar to or linked to each other, or issues being too far from realization to be plausible.

To counter possible scoring fatigue, or unconscious differences in scoring of issues near the start and end of a long list, the order in which issues were presented differed among the participants. Each individual's scores were used to rank the issues. The 35 issues with the highest median ranks, along with any comments, were retained for an in-person roundtable discussion.

After this initial scoring, participants were given the opportunity to retain any issues that they thought had been undervalued; one issue was retained during this process. A new issue that had emerged in the global news media during this period also was presented, yielding a new total of 37 issues for consideration.

Prior to the roundtable discussion, two participants were assigned to each of the issues (three to the newly suggested topic) to further investigate its novelty, likelihood of occurrence or implementation, and likely magnitude of positive or negative effects. During the roundtable, each topic was discussed in relation to the criteria for inclusion. The rank from the initial round of scoring, and the proportion of participants that were aware of the topic, were considered in the discussion.

During the discussion of some topics, the emphasis was adjusted, or additional points and sources of information were included. Following discussion of each topic, all participants independently and confidentially rescored the topic. In the end, the 15 conservation issues with the highest median ranks were selected and shared with the global conservation community. This annual scan provides expert analysis to researchers, environmentalists, NGOs, and policy makers to use in conducting further study and in preparing regulatory and legal action.

In 2019, Sutherland and colleagues published an assessment[3] to determine if awareness of, and involvement in, the issues identified in the first edition (2009) of the conservation horizon scan had changed. They consulted 12 leading conservation organizations. The assessment revealed that, in 2019, the conservation organizations were more aware of each and every one of the 15 issues flagged in the initial horizon scan than they were just a year after the initial scan was completed (2010). Further, the conservation organizations reported that they were as (or more) actively involved in two-thirds of issues in 2019 than they were in 2010. These findings seem to suggest that the yearly conservation horizon scan has been useful in identifying emerging issues of significance.

4. Map systems and explore drivers of change

The horizon scan provides you with important information about emerging changes and how they are manifesting themselves. The next step involves identifying what is driving those changes, and how they relate to each other within the system.

Systems mapping is an exercise which studies how key variables interact over time and form patterns of behaviors across an interconnected network. Systems evaluation specialist

Joelle Cook has led numerous strategic learning and evaluation projects for dozens of US-based not-for-profit organizations, and has written an accessible introduction to systems mapping.[4] Cook's guide includes tools to map a system's elements and connections, such as actor maps (which show the connections among people or organizations that are important players in a particular context); mind maps (a visual thinking tool that helps to organize information and show relationships among parts of the larger whole); issue maps (which diagram the issues and arguments around a core concern), and casual loop diagrams (which map how variables influence one another, helping to reveal a system's feedback structures and potential points of intervention).

Systems mapping can help in generating a consensus among those involved in a Foresight exercise on the elements within a system and how they relate to and impact each other. In short, it facilitates discovery of where change could occur.

Another tool used to ascertain and visualize drivers of change is the tiered cascade chart (or diagram). A cascade diagram allows one to explore the impact of change across different areas over time, and to visualize second, third and fourth order changes as one variable generates a consequence which, in turn, generates another consequence, and so on. Policy Horizons Canada provides a cascade diagram exercise for facilitators in its online Foresight training manual.[5] This exercise is designed to explore plausible future implications of a driver of change.

5. Prepare scenarios

Once the drivers of change have been revealed, scenario development begins. It is very common in Foresight exercises to elaborate three or four different scenarios in which the variables are adjusted for each future scenario. While the scenarios may vary greatly, each is plausible in its own right. They include aspects from recent history that continue to be relevant, like ongoing trends, as well as emerging phenomenon, like a technology that is coming out on to the market. Scenario development is increasingly being used to support planning and decision-making in conditions of uncertainty related to major global challenges like climate change.

Scenarios and the narratives around them are often presented in whole or in part by stories and images. A common scenario building exercise uses a 2x2 matrix, where two leading drivers are placed on one axis and two key themes of uncertainty are placed on another. Another commonly used method is cross-impact analysis, which shows the relationships between events and variables. The European Foresight Platform, cited in the "Where to learn more" section of Chapter 5, offers a helpful description of how to use cross-impact analysis.

The largest urban area in Northern California provides a good example of preparing alternative scenarios.[6] In 2018, the San Francisco Bay Area Planning and Urban Research Association (SPUR) launched a multiyear effort to develop a vision for the San Francisco Bay Area in the year 2070, along with the strategies needed to make the vision a reality. SPUR's Board of Directors, comprising more than 100 area business and civic leaders, undertook a scenario planning process to understand choices, chains of events, alternatives and possible outcomes to support better decision-making in the face of future uncertainty.

Board members used their annual retreat to develop a set of scenarios for the Bay Area in 2070. Working in small, facilitated breakout groups, they identified the most important forces shaping the future (that is, drivers of change) and considered their interplay. The process began with the belief that multiple futures are possible. Four critical uncertainties were explored: the economy, housing, transportation and the physical form of the region's urbanized areas.

SPUR described the four scenarios that emerged from the process as "myths of the future," stories that reveal the potential long-term outcomes of the choices made today. These scenarios reveal a wide variation in how circumstances will unfold in the decades ahead.

One scenario, Gated Utopia, is characterized by economic prosperity and social exclusion. The Bay Area of 2070 remains an innovation center and offers a great lifestyle – but only for those with money. A collective choice to *not* expand the housing supply, nor to make investments in other public forms of social support, has pushed all but the wealthy out of the region.

A second scenario, Bunker Bay Area, features a metropolis in economic decline and social exclusion. The Bay Area has balkanized into factions marked by extreme inequality and segregation. Trust between people is low and resources are scarce, making this a high-stress, low-satisfaction way of life for all. In this scenario, the Bay Area of 2070 is a place of declining economic opportunity. Slums surround small pockets of wealth concentrated in highly manicured and highly protected neighborhoods.

A third scenario, Rust Belt West, finds a Bay Area in economic decline. Activist communities promote inclusive measures that support poor people. The metropolis has forged an alternative economy where meeting basic needs is a struggle. A significant cultural shift has resulted in a strong sense of social solidarity, but resources have dwindled and quality of life has suffered.

The most optimistic of the four scenarios, A New Social Compact, envisions a socially inclusive Bay Area experiencing economic prosperity. There is an emphasis on economic growth as well as belief in society's ability to provide opportunity for all. This principle of shared prosperity has led to substantial investment in social housing, public transit, education and other foundations of an equitable society.

SPUR concluded the exercise with the declared intention to apply learnings from the scenario exercise to researching and developing recommendations that can set the Bay Area on a path to an economically strong, socially just and environmentally sustainable future. The scenarios, coupled with evocative drawings, provided an illustrative and communicative tool for working with a range of stakeholders.

In Chapter 4, I share several scenarios for plausible post-COVID-19 futures. These alternative futures, generated by Foresight specialists and others in the midst of the pandemic, provide food for thought to organizations trying to make sense of how the ongoing crisis will change the world in which we live.

6. Develop policy options

It is at this step that you begin to translate the results of a Foresight exercise into action. Examine the implications of each individual scenario, such as the risks, challenges, and opportunities. What do these scenarios mean for your organization, its mission and priorities, and the way that it conducts its work? Does your organization have the capacity to respond appropriately to each scenario? What do the scenarios mean for your staff, clients, and partners?

The purpose of Foresight is not only to inform, but also to stimulate action in response to the insights generated. By taking multiple scenarios into consideration when developing plans and strategies, governments can boost the quality of decision-making and improve service to the citizen and community.

Foresight findings are likely to spur thinking about fundamental changes in how your organization is staffed, structured, and directed. They can rock the boat by introducing unexpected ideas and perspectives not previously considered. This can be very unsettling and controversial, particularly if key stakeholders have not bought into the process. The surprises emerging from a Foresight exercise will be easier for your organization to handle if the process is transparent, participatory, and methodologically credible.

Once a Foresight exercise is completed, it should be shared and discussed with concerned parties, including decision-makers. Unless the work has been carried out for a confidential purpose, such as national defense planning, it ought to be made public if it is a government report. Decision-makers need to be given time to digest findings, which should be taken into consideration in the organization's planning and budget processes.

A rigorous Foresight process can mix and match methods in different ways, using ones that seem most relevant to the circumstances, including the time, expertise and budget available to carry out the work. The process of developing policy options gives rise to a further set of actions, including stakeholder consultation; assessing the costs and benefits of different policy choices; seeking approval for changes to rules, regulations and laws; making implementation arrangements; regular monitoring; and evaluation.

Chapter 3

International Examples of Foresight in Practice

In the previous chapter, I shared examples of Foresight tools being used by an international network of conservation experts, and an urban research organization in California. Chapter 3 expands on this pair of cases by exploring the applications of Foresight in several different country contexts.

Let's start with Kazakhstan, where in November 2019 about 30 officials from government and state-owned enterprises gathered in the country's largest city, Almaty, for a facilitated workshop exploring national development issues, alternative futures, and the use of future methods to improve long-run competitiveness. The workshop was financed by the Asian Development Bank (ADB), which in April 2020 published a report[1] featuring case studies of futures thinking and Foresight workshops in several developing Asian countries.

Participants in the Almaty workshop were divided into five groups tackling one topic each: infrastructure for agricultural development and beyond; tourism as a key contributor to economic growth; smart city applications to treat waste; Foresight for industrial and innovative development; and increasing competitiveness through regional cooperation.

The groups challenged "used futures" (an idea of the future created for another context and not necessarily well suited for the one being considered); anticipated disruptions in the year 2030; articulated the implications of these disruptions; created scenarios to manage uncertainty; developed the preferred vision; and created new metaphors or stories.

The workshop generated four alternative future scenarios for each of the five topics tackled. The workshop planted the seed of futures thinking within the government, and contributed to a growing cadre of Foresight champions. Since the workshop, the government has taken action in the topic areas that were deliberated. For example, in the area of infrastructure for agricultural development, the government is working with private sector partners to build a large, modern meat processing facility. On tourism, the government launched a new tourism campaign with videos that all use a variation of a catch phrase ("very nice") popularized internationally by the fictional Kazakh reporter Borat Sagdiyev, played by the British actor Sacha Baron Cohen.

The ADB report also describes the bank's support for a futures workshop held in Cambodia in September 2019. That workshop took place in the context of the Southeast Asian country's aspiration to become a digital economy by 2030, and an upper-middle-income country by 2050. The 30–35 government officials who participated in the workshop learned the concepts of used futures, emerging issues, and alternative futures, and how to influence and create the "preferred future." They chose six topics for discussion: transparency and accountability, leadership, women's empowerment, climate resilience, innovation, and technology in governance.

In an exercise employing Casual Layered Analysis, the government officials came up with several nature-related metaphors. For example, the group focused on leadership saw Cambodia today as "leap frogging" and future Cambodia as a fully grown tiger. Among the follow-up steps proposed was making futures thinking part of the civil service intake coursework.

A comprehensive look at future global risks

In several countries, Foresight is used extensively for strategy development related to national defense and security. In the US, the National Intelligence Council (NIC) employs a large team of analysts to assess the forces shaping the world. In 2017, the NIC published the latest edition of its quadrennial report on global trends and scenarios.[2]

Preparation of the report began two years earlier, when the NIC identified uncertainties and assumptions underlying US foreign policy. The agency conducted research and consulted with a plethora of experts in and outside of government to gain a better understanding of important trends, which it used to help identify broader global dynamics. The NIC then assessed implications of emerging trends over the next five years, and over a 20-year horizon.

Early in the process, the NIC reviewed bipartisan US planning assumptions since 1945 to identify those most (and least) likely to be in tension with the emerging strategic context. These exercises helped in the prioritization of issues, countries, and people to visit, and in managing the scope of research.

The NIC visited about 35 countries to seek ideas from more than 2500 people from various backgrounds and professions. Visits with senior officials and strategists worldwide informed the agency's understanding of the evolving strategic intent and national interests of major powers.

The agency corresponded with hundreds of natural and social scientists, thought leaders, religious figures, business and industry representatives, diplomats, development experts, and women, youth, and civil society organizations around the world. This research was supplemented by soliciting feedback on preliminary analysis through social media, at events like the South by Southwest Interactive Festival, and through traditional workshops and individual reviews of drafts. In considering geopolitical power, the report looked not just at gross domestic product and military spending, but also ideas and relationships, and the emergence of influential corporations, social movements and individuals.

Teams of experts "representing" key international actors

carried out analytic simulations to explore future paths for world regions, the international order, the security environment and the global economy. The process also included consideration of potential discontinuities in regions and topic areas that could lead to major shifts from the status quo. The report creatively presented these as fictional news articles from the future, such as "Bangladesh Climate Geoengineering Sparks Protest" (April 4, 2033), and "Gig Workers Riot in London and New York" (September 17, 2021).

Multiple scenarios were developed to imagine how important uncertainties might result in alternative futures. These scenarios explored the key choices that governments, organizations, and individuals might make in response to emerging trends that could realign existing trajectories, leading to opportunities to shape better futures.

The timing of the NIC's quadrennial report intentionally coincides with the inauguration of a new US presidential administration. The report provides incoming officials (as well as the general public) insights about future risks and opportunities in the global environment. By the time you have read this sentence, the NIC may have already published its new report (scheduled for release in early 2021).

Possible scenarios for delivery of international assistance

I have spent the past two decades working in international development. It is from this field that I have plucked the following example of how one donor country's foreign aid agency conducted a major Foresight initiative designed to explore possible long-term changes across the world.

In mid-2014, the French Development Agency (Agence Française de Développement, or AFD) initiated a Foresight exercise[3] designed as a collective organizational effort. Staff volunteered from the agency's offices in France as well as in field offices abroad. A comprehensive questionnaire was sent to all AFD personnel. Dozens of individuals from various sectors (e.g., banking, research, civil society) outside the organization were also consulted for their views on how the world would evolve over the coming years.

The first phase of the initiative was primarily organized around short workshops involving more than 400 persons in total. Participants identified drivers of change and AFD's key challenges up to 2025–2030. Hundreds of identified drivers were then analyzed to construct a "foresighting system," organized into five major fields and, within these fields, a total of 22 themes to structure the analysis.

The next step was creating theme-based working groups staffed by volunteers, who reviewed historical developments and analyzed major trends, uncertainties, possible upheavals, and weak signals with related, less perceptible signals. This analysis produced a set of Foresight files and assumptions on future changes for each of the themes.

About one year into the process, a smaller group began work on ensuring the consistency of the eighty-or-so assumptions. It constructed partial scenarios and then more comprehensive ones, with different global outlooks and trajectories. Ultimately, four scenarios were selected for the different questions that they raised, and their potential impacts on the activities of aid donors. Finally, the initiative queried what the practical consequences might be for AFD in the event of each scenario.

One of the scenarios, titled Impasse, depicts a world where ecological tipping points have been reached, leading to a series of crises around the planet. Another, Babel 3.0, is a future world torn by severe economic, environmental, political and social tensions, and where prosperous regions exist alongside highly fragile zones.

The results of the AFD Foresight exercise were shared widely within the agency and deliberated by leadership as it planned strategy for the years ahead.

Foresight expertise at the center of Singapore's government

Among the world's leading central government Foresight units is Singapore's Centre for Strategic Futures (CSF). CSF serves as a think tank responsible for developing future scenarios from a whole-of-government perspective. Its roots trace back to the creation of an office in the Prime Minister's Office to develop scenarios. Even earlier, in the 1980s, the Ministry of Defense experimented with future planning efforts.

Today, CSF carries out open-ended research, usually with a 10- to 20-year time frame. The specialized team informs public policy thinking, discovers blind spots, and encourages more robust decision-making. Building on more than four decades of government Foresight work, CSF scans for small or local innovation or disruption that has the potential to grow in scale or geographic distribution. It works extensively with scenario planning.

CSF performs in-depth examinations of emerging issues to understand the implications for public policy and communicate them to stakeholders. Recent examples include the rising popularity of new eco-friendly alternatives to conventional burial and cremation, implications for young workers of Baby Boomers remaining in their jobs well into their 60s, and the growing popularity of digital therapies for stress and anxiety.

CSF also builds the capacity for conducting Foresight across the public service, and helps the public policy community in Singapore rethink existing assumptions, stress-test current policies, and develop new strategies as context changes.

Visioning EU customs in 2040

The EU Policy Lab, and the European Commission's Directorate General for Taxation and Customs Union, recently used

Foresight to develop understanding of the trends and drivers impacting the EU Customs ecosystem, as well as possible paths for how this system could evolve by 2040. The organizers of the process[4] used a range of methods, including horizon scanning, a Real-time Delphi survey, scenario building, visioning and roadmapping.

In a series of blogs, the EU Policy Lab reported on how the process unfolded, including what happened at workshops organized as part of the exercise. The blogs, accompanied by process descriptions and photographs, provide a great perspective on how to run Foresight workshops.

In February 2019, organizers held a scoping workshop to understand the ecosystem of the EU customs union, and key actors within it. The workshop involved 20 people from the "EU customs world," including EU institutions, customs administrations, and trade associations. Participants worked collaboratively to describe this world in detail on a physical canvas which comprised five layers: actors and stakeholders, infrastructure, regulation and governance, external and international issues, and money flows. The workshop generated a shared understanding of the EU customs world.

Subsequent workshops were held to identify the key drivers of change that will affect the future evolution of customs in the EU up to 2040, as well as the main uncertainties affecting them, and the co-creation of four scenarios representing four different futures. Keeping the key stakeholders involved from the very beginning of the process enabled the collaborative creation of detailed scenario narratives, presenting plausible futures relevant to the customs world – understood and accepted by all.

Workshops also were used to: i) customize a Foresight tool called the Scenario Exploration System, ii) create a shared vision for EU customs, and, at the last workshop, iii) engage high-level representatives of all EU customs administrations to embrace the vision, and begin collective reflection on what the vision could imply for future policy action.

This Foresight exercise painted a picture of a future EU Customs Union in which customs authorities work to protect society, the environment and the EU economy through facilitation of trade and risk-based supervision of supply chains; proactively work with stakeholders in a seamless fashion; commit to innovation and sustainability while serving as a global reference for customs; and act together in a unified fashion.

The exercise contributed to adoption of a concrete policy measure – in this case, the EU Customs Union Action Plan.[5] Launched in September 2020, the action plan will be used to ensure an integrated European approach to customs risk management that supports effective controls by EU Member States. Further it will assist customs authorities in developing more effective risk management, promoting compliance, managing e-commerce, and ensuring that customs authorities act as one.

Getting a handle on global risks to food security

Food safety is a major concern for consumers, producers, and governments around the world. This is why the Food and Agriculture Organization (FAO) was created 75 years ago to lead international efforts to defeat hunger and improve nutrition and food security. In October 2013, the FAO organized a technical workshop in Italy on early warning systems and horizon scanning around food safety.

Workshop participants included representatives of national agencies that had been using Foresight methodologies since the 1980s or early 1990s, including the Canadian Food Inspection Agency, the European Food Safety Authority, the UK Department for Environment, Food and Rural Affairs (in collaboration with Cranfield University) and the UK Food Standards Agency.

FAO recognized that different kinds of surveillance

approaches and tools are regularly used to identify and assess food security-related hazards, risks and issues and to provide recommendations for potential actions. While these traditional approaches are reasonably effective in identifying immediate hazards and issues; FAO had determined that there is a need to also take into account important medium- to long-term issues to facilitate preventative actions.

It was felt that Foresight could improve strategic planning by identifying specific emerging risks and opportunities, and by monitoring how the food safety context is changing over time. Key drivers identified as affecting the context were globalization of trade, climate change, scientific progress, and urbanization.

Ahead of the workshop, the FAO prepared a paper[6] on horizon scanning and Foresight methods used in relation to food safety, and on the use of horizon scanning and Foresight across FAO units. The paper, and the workshop discussions, were then used to inform decisions on how Foresight methodologies, including horizon scanning, could be used in FAO efforts to promote food safety.

Subsequently, in 2017, international experts on food and agriculture launched an international collaborative initiative, Foresight4Food. The initiative aims to provide a mechanism for better analysis and synthesis of key trends and possible futures in global food systems and to support more informed and strategic dialogue between the private sector, government, science and civil society. Foresight4Food promotes Foresight analysis of food systems and improves linkages between scientific analysis and policy dialogue with stakeholders.

The initiative is supporting the work of existing institutions and platforms dealing with food and agriculture issues by coordinated efforts providing Foresight services and analysis to serve multiple purposes and groups. Donor resources have been secured to support the initiative and its engagement with a range of actors, platforms and networks possessing an interest in Foresight for food systems. Foresight4 Food is studying rural poverty, food system risks, and food system recovery pathways out of the COVID-19 pandemic.

Exploring the future of migration

The OECD is an active user and promoter of Foresight. Its Strategic Foresight Unit supports use of Foresight across OECD directorates and committees, and coordinates a global network of Foresight experts from OECD member governments. The Paris-based organization has published several Foresight knowledge products, including a paper[7] on developing migration and integration policies for the year 2035. To produce the paper, a task force comprising government officials from ministries with migration responsibilities in several Western European countries, Canada and Japan collaborated with experts of the OECD Secretariat, academe and civil society.

This Foresight exercise involved a literature review of Foresight studies related to migration and integration, analysis of pertinent global trends, horizon scanning, and identification of signals of change. Megatrends affecting migration and integration of migrants were identified: environmental changes and extreme weather, geopolitical instability and conflict, and aging of populations. Uncertainties were also flagged: technological change, change in the purpose of migration and migrant integration, new stakeholders, and shifting migration directions.

Three Foresight workshops were held to develop eight scenarios, grouped under four broad themes based on a collective exercise among the stakeholders participating in the workshops. Opportunities and challenges arising from the scenarios were explored, as were policy implications.

The scenarios that resulted from the exercise were then discussed by the OECD Working Party on Migration, which consists of government officials engaged in establishing national policies on immigration in OECD member countries.

Looking ahead in the battle against HIV/AIDS

The final example in this chapter is provided by the Joint United Nations Programme on HIV and AIDS (UNAIDS). In 2005, this UN body, which promotes coordinated global action on HIV/ AIDS, used a participatory process to elaborate three scenarios[8] for the AIDS epidemic in Africa twenty years in the future (that is, in 2025).

Hundreds of people, mostly Africans living and working in Africa, and involved in the fight against AIDS, contributed to the scenarios building exercise. Artists, writers, supporting institutions, and experts from several other fields contributed to the effort with analysis and comments.

The scenarios were built on two major assumptions, and some key uncertainties. The assumptions were that AIDS would still be affecting Africa in two decades' time, and that decisions taken at the time of the report would shape the continent's future history. The uncertainties included how the AIDS crisis is perceived, and by whom; would there be incentive and capacity to deal with the crisis; would the then-prevailing level of interest in the issue be sustained; and would the incentive and resources available for addressing AIDS and its impact be sufficient to meet the need.

Five forces were identified as drivers of Africa's AIDS pandemic: the growth or erosion of unity and integration; the evolution of beliefs, values, and meanings; the leveraging of resources and capabilities; the generation and application of knowledge; and the distribution of power and authority. The scenarios were created from the interplay of these drivers, and illustrated by regional epidemiological stories.

One scenario, dubbed Tough Choices: Africa takes a Stand, relates a story of African leaders taking tough measures that curtail the spread of AIDS, thereby laying the foundation for future growth and development and reduction in the incidence of HIV. Governments insist that HIV and AIDS be tackled as part of a broad, coherent strategy for medium-to-long-term development. For this scenario, and the other two scanarios, estimates were provided for the number of people with AIDS, and for spending to tackle the disease.

Another scenario – Traps and Legacies: The Whirlpool – sees Africa tethered to negative legacies and AIDS exacerbating poverty. The scenario identifies seven legacies, or traps, that prevent effective, long-term, or widespread development on the continent. This tragic scenario depicts a world where AIDS motivates people and institutions into a response to the crisis, but finds them stymied from making progress due to shrinking capacities and infrastructure.

The final scenario, Times of Transition: Africa Overcomes, envisions what might happen if a coherent, integrated development response is adopted to address HIV and AIDS in Africa. The scenario is presented as the account of a storyteller and her friends as they look back in time to 2025 from the vantage point of 2036. The scenario describes six interlocking transformations that reshape the continent's future. Action taken in health, development, trade, security, and international relations lead to substantial progress in tackling the AIDS crisis.

Chapter 4

Scenarios for the Post-Pandemic World

The pandemic and economic crisis that began in 2020 has upended plans and strategies for governments and businesses around the world. The costs associated with the ongoing crisis blew a large hole in public budgets, and affected every layer of government and the government interface with the private sector and individual citizens. Companies had to rethink strategy on the fly and make difficult decisions based on incomplete information and under extreme pressure. Many companies will continue to struggle in search of a way forward. Others will join the many businesses that have already closed.

In this time of crisis and disruptive change, Foresight practitioners have found a receptive audience for their expertise and advice. Many leaders, taken aback by recent events, perceive an urgent need to get a better handle on disruptive trends and risks in order to make their organizations more resilient and agile. The crisis will not "be wasted" if they seize the moment to adopt good habits, like challenging assumptions, testing hypotheses, encouraging more participatory decision-making, and crafting (and preparing for) plausible alternative futures.

Stefano Oliveri, Digital Transformation Director at Schnieder Electric, views Foresight as one of the key skills we must learn in the wake of COVID-19, arguing that the future should be integrated into what we do and what we think, like reading and writing.[1] By embracing Foresight, organizations expand their opportunities to improve internal practices and open up possibilities not envisioned before the pandemic. Foresight will also help decision-makers gain insights into how changing practices and new developments during the pandemic are interacting with pre-existing megatrends to shape a different tomorrow than one imagined before COVID-19 and its consequences came to dominate our lives.

Several futurists, Foresight practitioners, strategy specialists, researchers, and consulting firms have shared analysis and commentary on the changes they expect to see in the world in the coming years. This chapter highlights a selection of the scenarios that they have developed.

In the first half of 2020, governments with strong central Foresight units quickly turned their attention to the pandemic and its potential implications. For example, Singapore's CSF began examining where COVID-19 was impacting existing trends or introducing new ones, how these trends were interacting, and what uncertainties were emerging. CSF then articulated five ways in which the pandemic will reshape the world in the medium to long term, and create shifts in the observed environment.[2]

The five identified shifts were:

1. Globalization may change in nature, but not retreat.
2. Structure of economies could be fundamentally altered.
3. New innovations and increasing digitalization will birth unintended consequences.
4. Socio-economic inequalities will deepen and new ones will be created.
5. Relationships between governments, businesses and citizens will be reshaped.

CSF's assessments were informed by signals observed during the pandemic, ideas put forth by experts and commentators, internal workshops, including with the broader futures community within the government, and discussions with external interlocutors.

In addition to promoting discussion of broader shifts with global implications, CSF prepared issue briefs focusing on a specific topic and plausible trajectories, and highlighting public policy questions for Singapore.

CSF's work during the crisis stimulated government-wide dialogue about the alternative futures that the city-state might have to confront, and how best to do so, and in the process contributed to more robust policy-making.

The following six examples of post-pandemic scenario development were formulated outside of government. Most of them have a time range that is much shorter than a typical Foresight exercise (i.e., a handful of years rather than decades). They were all completed before the distribution of COVID-19 vaccines began.

From Downward Accelerator to a New Renaissance

The Atlantic Council's Foresight, Strategy, Risks Initiative identifies key global trends and uncertainties in an effort to chart pathways to a more prosperous, stable, and peaceful future. Matthew J. Burrows, the initiative's director, and Peter Engelke, a senior fellow at the initiative, have undertaken a preliminary examination[3] of the geopolitical implications of the COVID-19 crisis.

They developed three short-to-medium term scenarios emerging from the crisis to help improve long-term decision-making by the US and its allies at a time of major uncertainty in a complex and volatile environment. The approach they took puts a heavy emphasis on how COVID-19 affects geopolitics and the balance of world powers.

This study highlighted several prospects for the pandemic, including rising death tolls as the virus spreads to the developing world; mutation of the coronavirus complicating vaccine development; a difficult and extended economic recovery; continued deglobalization; a disproportionate impact on vulnerable and disadvantaged populations in the US; and a possible sharp decline in American soft power if the country is seen to be struggling to manage the virus or failing to provide help to partners abroad.

Building on these observations, and an assessment of how the crisis could affect various major countries and world regions, Burrows and Engelke provide three scenarios over the first half of the current decade. They start with the most pessimistic, The Great Downward Accelerator.

Under this scenario, the US, Europe and China struggle as recovery stretches well into the decade due to the long time it takes to develop a vaccine. The US and China continue to experience economic and trade conflict, while EU institutions become paralyzed as divisions deepen between EU member states in the north and south of Europe. Deglobalization speeds up, leading to slow economic growth globally, rising poverty levels in the developing world, and the potential of open conflict between the US and a China-Russia alliance.

The second scenario, named China First, envisions expansion of Chinese support to infrastructure projects in the developing world as part of an effort to undermine the credibility of Western liberal democracy. Within China, the Communist Party galvanizes public support by depicting Western democracies as unable to meet the challenge of the pandemic, and continues to suppress internal dissent.

Meanwhile, in the US, socialism gains ground, yet President Trump is re-elected after stirring up anti-China fervor. The US and Europe institute wealth taxes and draw closer to counter China's growing influence. American allies in Asia resist an alliance against China since they have become more economically dependent on it. Much of the world perceives an America in decline, contributing to China's growing geopolitical stature.

(*Note: The above scenario was developed before former US President Donald Trump lost in his bid for re-election. The fact that one event in a particular scenario does not come to pass does not necessarily mean that other aspects of the scenario will similarly fail to be realized.*)

This second scenario further envisions growing chaos in other world regions, including food riots in the Middle East and North Africa, a Shia rebellion in Saudi Arabia and Bahrain, and Chinese-funded Russian intervention to provide food aid and reinforce authoritarian rulers. More hopefully, this scenario depicts the United Nations assessing that reduced greenhouse gas emissions would keep the global temperature rise to between 1.5 and 2.0 degrees Celsius.

The final scenario developed by Burrows and Engelke pictures a New Renaissance, in which the US rallies leading economic powers to reach agreement on a coordinated pandemic recovery plan, including the removal of border closures and trade barriers. The global economy slowly gains steam, leading to a V-shaped recovery. The G20 ensures that the entire world population is vaccinated at no charge, boosting market confidence. The scenario also has the G20 calling for the creation of a warning agency on disease, conflict, and climate. In the US, President Trump loses his bid for re-election.

Other major developments under this final scenario include China permanently closing its wild animal markets and enforcing new laws prohibiting livestock in dense urban areas. China also agrees to participate in the new warning agency, which receives the backing of the US Congress. The EU, US and China come together to deal with global challenges, even as the US remains concerned about Chinese influence through the Belt and Road Initiative. As tensions ease among leading powers, the world economy resumes growth and attainment of the Sustainable Development Goals appears within reach.

Four scenarios for business leaders

The management consultancy Deloitte Consulting LLP, and Salesforce, the cloud-based software company, have published four scenarios[4] shortly after the pandemic began to take hold in the US. The scenarios show different ways in which the pandemic could speed up or shift the course of social and business changes over the next 3 to 5 years (that is, up to April 2025). Deloitte and Salesforce prepared their scenarios report to give business leaders a chance to explore potential long-term implications of COVID-19, and provide them with a window in which they could act to strengthen organizational resilience.

The report identifies five key uncertainties likely to generate impacts following the pandemic: the severity of COVID-19 and how it spreads; collaboration within and between countries; response of the healthcare system; the pandemic's economic impacts; and the level of social cohesion. The authors argue that the first and last of these uncertainties will drive the overall impact of COVID-19.

The four distinct scenarios, based on current trends and critical uncertainties, are labeled Passing Storm, Lone Wolves, Good Company, and Sunrise in the East. Each scenario is described in terms of impact on society, technology, economy, environment and politics.

In the Passing Storm, social cohesion grows; advances in technology continue apace; the economy enters a recession, exacerbating inequality; global collaboration on the environment increases; and trust in politics is strengthened, with bodies like the World Health Organization becoming more relevant.

A darker Lone Wolves scenario features xenophobia and declining social cohesion; growing use of technology for surveillance and control; economic turmoil and supply chain disruption; reduced attention to the environment as countries move toward greater energy independence; and increased isolation in the political sphere as governments turn inward to tackle the pandemic domestically.

Good Company finds society becoming more purpose-driven, and big companies striving toward solutions in areas such as health tech and biotech. Power becomes more concentrated among large firms with mixed trends in the environment. Some companies invest in renewables, and governments increasingly partner with business to jointly pursue solutions.

The fourth scenario, Sunshine in the East, finds governments around the world looking to Asia for guidance since Asian countries have successfully managed COIVD-19. More attention is given to the "good of the whole," and increased data-sharing enables advances in artificial intelligence and other technological capabilities. The drawn-out pandemic causes economies to shrink, resulting in less concern for the environment relative to economic recovery.

The report's authors state their intent to challenge expectations and to stimulate new ideas about the future. They also pose questions to readers, such as whether a particular scenario is being ignored, what would have to be done differently to succeed under different scenarios, and what should be learned about different capabilities and partnerships.

From a Global Market Place to Walled Gardens

The International Institute for Management Development (IMD) is a globally recognized business school in Lausanne, Switzerland. It has published a report[5] proposing four plausible scenarios for the post-pandemic world. Compared to other scenarios featured in this chapter, the IMD approach gives special attention to digital technology.

The report identifies three factors that create the greatest impact and uncertainty in the post-pandemic world: 1) longevity of the virus; 2) how the population's view of economic, political and social boundaries will be affected (people's mindsets); and 3) how consumers will respond to the digital tools and technologies that have emerged due to COVID-19. By examining how these factors could impact each other, IMD elaborated four different plausible future scenarios for the purpose of challenging thinking and assumptions.

In one scenario, named Global Marketplace, COVID-19 is a

passing health event and widely recognized as such. Impacts are minimal, and people seek to return to business. Border restrictions are lifted and trade picks up again. The use of digital technologies during the pandemic leads to a new wave of global digital innovation. More people begin to live and work in other countries.

A second scenario, Digital Reset, pictures a world in which the number of infections and deaths from the virus does not decline. National governments realize that unilateral responses are failing, so a massive multilateral effort is undertaken to slow the spread of the virus. After some time and effort, progress is made, and a large part of the success is credited to the globally coordinated response. Travel restrictions are removed, tourism picks up quickly, and global supply chains are reopened. People realize that the pandemic was made much worse because of the constant flow of sensationalized misinformation. Therefore, many reduce their exposure to digital media and generally retreat from an over-exposure to digital technologies.

Another scenario, Back to Basics, presents a world where COVID-19 infections and deaths fail to slow down, causing people to become distrustful and skeptical about threats from outside their immediate environments. Tourism fails to reignite, as people choose to travel close to home, and global supply chains are dismantled to avoid vulnerabilities to future shocks. Suspicion grows of people and products from other parts of the world. Digital technologies become too invasive and pervasive for many, leading to disengagement. Even young people spend less time online.

The last scenario in IMD's report is called Walled Gardens. In this case, the immediate threat of infection and death disappears in most parts of the world, yet lingering suspicions remain about the dangers of pandemics from foreign lands. A local-first, isolationist mentality takes hold in the US and elsewhere as nations prioritize themselves over the broader global interest. National patriotism grows along with pressure to limit immigration. Foreign tourism destinations lose their allure and local trips and events become more popular. Technology remains pervasive but people become less interested in global themes and celebrities. Local versions of global apps and software products make gains against the digital giants.

The IMD report concludes with the introduction of a five-step process for readers to organize scenario planning sessions in which teams assess and debate multiple scenarios.

What lies ahead for the US?

Carol Dumaine, a former US intelligence community analyst, and Stanley Feder, a research political scientist and senior analyst in the US intelligence community, have developed alternative scenarios and implications of the COVID-19 crisis for the US up to 2023.[6] As a starting point for their work, they interviewed economists, scientists, science writers, political scientists, former senior government officials, and journalists, asking each to identify which uncertainties would have the most impact on shaping the near future.

Taking into consideration the feedback they received from interviewees, Dumaine and Feder chose the following uncertainties as the basis for elaborating three scenarios: 1) society's ability to cope with fear and uncertainty; 2) how society views the trade-off between maximizing business profits and maximizing human welfare; and 3) the degree to which tribalism divides and weakens social cohesion. The four resulting scenarios, briefly described below, are named Dickens' America, Politics of Responsibility, Grifters without a Plan, and Big Tent USA.

In Dickens' America, decision-makers deny and ignore the virus, while society at large is scared and simultaneously distracted and misinformed in a divided information environment filled with corporate-fed false information. Businesses require their employees to come to work despite the continuing risk to their heath and the health of their families. Industry consolidates, the middle class dissipates, and small businesses lose their markets. Protections for workers and consumers are lacking, and COVID-19 overburdens health and local government systems.

Under the Politics of Responsibility scenario, the US takes action against economic inequality and government, community leaders and the public incorporate climate and other risks into economic valuation and into business practices and protections for everyone. A new US administration prioritizes economic and civil rights and enters into burden-sharing networks internationally and at home. A widely shared vision and independent media rally public support.

The bleak Grifters without a Plan scenario depicts a US that has become an oligarchic fascist state lacking a middle class. Society is fractured and fearful in an environment characterized by tribalism, prejudice and a media generating alternative truths. The public is pessimistic about the future and does not believe what it hears from the government and the media. Work has become scarce and food security widespread. The regime in power has no plan for the future and the country is on an unsustainable course as democratic states steer clear of the US.

Finally, Big Tent USA finds that COVID-19 has united Americans in isolationism as other countries shun the country due to its high infection rate and aggressive patriotism. Nongovernment organizations and government leaders stimulate optimism in a fearful public. Competent people are brought into the public administration at all levels of government as the country tackles internet vulnerabilities, upgrades infrastructure, and pursues economic self-sufficiency.

The analysts Dumaine and Feder state that while none of these scenarios is likely to emerge exactly as portrayed, parts of more than one of them could appear in our actual future. They encourage use of the scenarios to try and understand current signals of change, and to formulate adaptive strategies that strengthen readiness for whatever developments may emerge.

How Futurists see the world emerging from COVID-19

Rohit Talwar and fellow futurists and future-thinkers have produced four scenarios for 2022–2023 to help individuals and businesses prepare for life after the pandemic.[7] To develop the scenarios, they identified the most important and uncertain driving forces, including the evolution of the pandemic (from poorly contained to total eradication), and the shape of the recovery (from a deep, prolonged downturn to a strong rebound). The scenarios considered the possible impacts of these drivers on health, political, business, consumer sentiment, socio-demographic, science and technology, and environmental factors.

In one scenario, The Long Goodbye, COVID-19 is poorly contained and the economic downturn is deep and prolonged. Places most affected by the virus veer in and out of lockdown, and countries are afraid of opening their borders to visitors from infected countries. There is slow acknowledgement of the need for a global solution, though by mid-2021 a multi-stakeholder coalition comes together around a recovery plan. Wealthier countries help those in need of assistance and reform. A vaccine comes out in 2022 and is rolled out worldwide by the end of the following year.

(*Note: Although we now know that COVID-19 vaccines began to be distributed in late 2020, it is expected that vaccinations will continue into 2022 and beyond, with developing countries generally receiving shipments later than wealthy countries.*)

The VIP Economy portrays a vibrant economic rebound in the midst of a poorly contained pandemic. Countries with the resources are the first to benefit from testing and vaccinations, and strong physical distancing measures are put in place in many countries to protect the middle and upper classes from the risk of infection from poorer people living in densely populated areas. Governments in developed countries prioritize healthcare for those most likely to drive the economic recovery. Meanwhile, in many developing countries, governments separate some populations from the rest and leave them to their fate.

In the Safe but Hungry scenario, public pressure causes health to be rated as more important than economic recovery. Testing, treatment and vaccinations are prioritized. Protective measures are imposed on businesses and public transport. Businesses where people tend to gather (like cinemas and restaurants) remain closed or repurpose themselves. Although the recovery is slower, it gives the impression of being more inclusive and sustainable.

Under the most optimistic scenario, Inclusive Abundance, COVID-19 is brought under control and the economy bounces back. Those in power speed the adoption of widespread testing, treatment and vaccination. Countries come together around the Sustainable Development Goals, providing help to the weakest countries. Efforts are made to provide all nations with technology to improve lives. Guaranteed basic incomes and services support the needy as they skill up to improve their job prospects.

Will the US be alright by 2022?

The Millennium Project, a global think tank with nodes in 67 countries, has developed a set of post-pandemic scenarios[7] at the request of the American Red Cross. The scenarios describe how the pandemic may evolve in the US between October 2020 to January 2022.

The exercise involved a review of other COVID-19 scenarios and the conduct of five Real-time Delphi studies. More than 250 medical doctors, public health professionals, emergency relief staff, economists and futurists provided inputs into the studies, which informed the elaboration of three scenarios. The scenarios were then subjected to external peer review before drafts were finalized.

The report's first scenario is labeled America Endures, and presents a case where the virus does not go away soon. Recession in the US leads to depression in many world regions. Political support for addressing the economic and business impacts of the pandemic is irregular, and natural disasters and food shortages stretch public services. Persistence of the pandemic has depressed the nation's morale. A local sense of community has grown as has use of digital technologies. People develop resistance, vaccines become more effective, immunity spreads, and the US moves toward universal health coverage.

Under the next scenario – Depression, Hubris, and Discord – the US has failed to adopt coherent strategies and policies to address the pandemic's threats, leading to a massive death toll. Hopes are low for a proven and effective vaccine. Inflation soars to 10%, bankruptcies are widespread, long lines form at food banks and jobless centers, and inequality grows. Crime and suicide rates are high and consideration is given to deploying troops and declaring martial law. Rationing of commodities might be introduced.

The final scenario, Things Went Right!, envisions successful control of the pandemic due to comprehensive action by a new administration in Washington, DC. Yet it was not until the death toll reached 450,000 that consensus grew around a science and policy-driven plan to overcome the pandemic. Medical innovations and vaccines emerged, and good coordination ensured that their use could be maximized. The US resumes collaboration with the WHO and major world economies. The one single factor that makes the greatest difference is social cohesion, which the country realizes is key to solving other problems.

The Millennium Project report identified key insights from

the three scenarios: the worst is yet to come; the situation in January 2022 could be substantially better or worse depending on actions taken in the latter part of 2020 and early 2021; a vaccine will not end the pandemic; and a combination of a whole-of-nation strategy, responsible public behavior, strategic leadership, and international coordination can greatly improve conditions.

More post-pandemic scenarios to ponder

The aforementioned scenarios for a post-pandemic world are a subset of the many scenarios that have been developed by various groups since the pandemic began. To view additional scenarios, check out the bibliography assembled by The Red (Team) Analysis Society, a consultancy devoted to anticipatory intelligence, strategic foresight, and warning and risk management for political and geopolitical uncertainty: https://www.redanalysis.org/2020/07/03/scenarios-for-covid-19-and-post-covid-19-worlds-a-bibliography/.

In addition, the OECD has produced a list of uncertainties and possible developments that could arise as COVID-19 further impacts and interacts with different human and natural systems. This list is accompanied by a selection of Foresight publications related to COVID-19: http://www.oecd.org/coronavirus/policy-responses/strategic-foresight-for-the-covid-19-crisis-and-beyond-using-futures-thinking-to-design-better-public-policies-c3448fa5/#:~:text=Abstract,the%20face%20of%20high%20uncertainty.

The post-pandemic scenarios described in this chapter are being digested by business leaders worried about their companies' prospects, and by government officials obliged to respond to a suffering population and struggling businesses. The range of alternative scenarios gives decision-makers and planners meaningful analysis to consider in preparing for different eventualities.

Chapter 5

Conclusion and Resources

Foresight is a valuable asset for organizations that want to improve their preparedness, competitiveness, and resiliency in an increasingly uncertain world of rapid change. What steps can you and your organization take to benefit from what Foresight has to offer?

Identify resources

What staff and budget can you harness to make Foresight a regular part of your organization? Can you assign someone as the Foresight focal point, and provide them with support? More and more organizations are including Foresight and futures thinking as part of a designated staff member's job description. Reserve funds in your very next budget for identifying weak signals, pinpointing trends, identifying drivers of change, and elaborating scenarios.

Revisit what you think you know

Challenge the assumptions underpinning your operational plans, policies and strategies. Are they valid? The intertwined health and economic crises have dramatically altered the way that many businesses operate, and have stimulated government spending, new public programs, and the adoption or revision of rules, regulations and legislation. Meanwhile, underlying trends – many related to digital technologies – have in some cases accelerated during the pandemic. If your previous assumptions are wrong, your existing plans of action need to be updated.

Start scanning

Begin a systematic scan of developments in and around the

environment in which your organization operates. Be alert to changes that could have a domino effect. When Indian officials issued stay-at-home orders to urban residents to limit the spread of the virus, many people in the informal economy lost their livelihoods. Millions of jobless migrants returned to rural areas, infecting local populations in areas with weaker health services. Public authorities in many jurisdictions have encouraged the wearing of facemasks to reduce transmission of the virus. As a result, millions of tons of used masks, and other personal protective equipment, like gloves, have clogged sewers and water treatment facilities, and added to ocean pollution.

In the US, 52% of adults between the ages of 18 and 29 were living with their parents in July 2020, a record high. The sudden new living arrangements produced a multitude of negative knock-on effects for various businesses, including landlords, insurance agencies, furniture and appliance vendors, and stores selling kitchen wares and utensils.

Make sure that the scanning work you do includes a mechanism to flag early warnings of change that could affect your organization's mandate, operations, and client relations.

Skill up

Learn more about Foresight and how it can help you achieve your goals by tapping into the informational and training resources identified in the "Where to learn more" section of this chapter (keep reading). If you have the budget, get your staff into a quality course on Foresight. Now is the time to develop your futures literacy.

Modify the planning process

Incorporate Foresight methodologies into your budgetary, planning and strategy development cycles, and schedule regular, structured team discussions on what internal horizon scanning has uncovered. Learn from the shock we have lived through by developing plausible scenarios of the future, including ones that involve cataclysmic events.

During the pandemic, we have often heard people express the wish for "things to return to normal." Yet in a sense, we are already there – normal times will continue to involve disruption driven by demographic trends, growing inequality, increased automation, scientific discoveries, and responses of a natural environment that has been very mistreated by humankind.

Make yours a learning organization

As you collect information, perform analysis, and generate insights, make sure that knowledge is disseminated within the organization and incorporated into onboarding, training, and staff guidance. It is not a surprise that organizations putting a high value on knowledge management are more likely to use Foresight.

Be ready to transform

Lay the groundwork for a thorough Foresight exercise that asks big questions relevant to your organization's mission, role, approaches, and environment. Be prepared for discoveries that could lead to strategic reallocation of resources and reordering of priorities in response to the outcomes of a comprehensive assessment of plausible future scenarios.

Finding our bearings with Foresight

Use of Foresight has increased in recent years and has further accelerated during the spread of COVID-19 and the resulting economic crisis. In early January 2020, before the virus ravaged Europe, the Government of Spain created a National Office for Foresight and Long-Term Country Strategy in the Presidency's Cabinet. The establishment of this new unit was inspired by similar units set up by governments in Europe and North America, as well as in international organizations.

Explaining the rationale for this new the unit, the director of the Prime Minister's Cabinet said, "One of the great defects of democracy is short-termism. In the frenetic daily life of governments, the urgent often overshadows the important. This in turn generates other problems such as [a] lack [of] strategic thinking,... legislative obsolescence, untapped opportunities or short anticipation, which are at the base of phenomena such as climate change, rural emptying or the loss of economic relevance for a nation."[1]

In September 2020, the European Union issued its first annual Strategic Foresight Report, presenting the strategy of the European Commission to integrate Foresight into EU policymaking. The report identified early lessons from the COVID-19 crisis, introduced resilience as a new compass for EU policymaking, and described the role of Foresight in strengthening the resilience of the EU and its member states.

In October 2020, the acting administrator of the US Agency for International Development announced that his organization would create a strategic foresight unit. He explained that creating such a unit would allow his agency's headquarters, "to scan the horizon for future crises and prepare us for uncertain and complex operating environments." He added that supporting field missions with scenario planning would make them "more responsive and more adaptive."[2]

These recent initiatives highlight how government bodies have grasped that while change has always been a fact of life, the pace of change around us has accelerated. Engineering, scientific and technological discoveries and innovations will reshape economies and governance systems, and greatly influence relations among peoples and nations. Growing wealth concentration, democratic backsliding, and declining trust in major institutions are also contributing to instability.

Artificial intelligence, including machine learning and facial recognition systems, virtual and augmented reality, automation of production and service delivery, genetic engineering and synthetic biology, laboratory-grown food, and the internet of things are among the trends that will dramatically alter our lives, including how we work, what we do with our leisure time, and our relationship with government and other power centers. The world stands to benefit greatly from some of these changes, but they also have implications for privacy, civil liberties, human rights, equality, and livelihoods. Ethical and moral standards are being challenged.

In addition, humanity has a broken relationship with nature. Deforestation, rampant consumption, pollution, species extinction, biodiversity loss, and climate change all threaten survival of the planet, humankind, and all living things. These problems have gotten worse, not better, in modern times.

During this ongoing period of unprecedented disruptive change, Foresight can help us find our balance and gain insight into what tomorrow could bring. As all-consuming as the current crisis has been, we would be wise to begin a regular, systematic assessment of plausible futures that will surely include other big shocks to the system.

In these unsettling times, Futurist Richard Laipo Lum counsels that, "our Foresight efforts should try to account for not just the surface-level implications of recent disruptions like the pandemic, but also how these recent events are interacting with the long-run transformations that were already underway. Foresight work that just thinks about COVID-19 as a stand-alone health crisis or only looks at the immediate responses to racial injustice conversations will fail to explore how these sudden shocks will interact with the several, deeper and longer-run changes that are stressing fundamental assumptions about society."[3]

A crisis is an ideal time to make improvements within an organization. Internal resistance to doing things differently tends to melt away in the midst of radically altered circumstances.

If your organization is a staid or traditional body, it may approach Foresight with some trepidation. But future-proofing your organization's plans and policies may determine success or failure as the pandemic recedes. The disruptions that are rattling the world will become more pronounced, not less. For this reason, your organization needs to be agile, adopt a growth mindset, and instill a culture of learning. By systematically performing the work required to discern plausible alternative futures, and then taking action to prepare for such futures, a forward-looking organization takes control of its destiny. Let that organization be yours.

Where to learn more

There are several sources to turn to for quality learning materials and basic training on Foresight.

Consistent with the aim of this book to spread awareness of Foresight – including to organizations with limited budgets – the informational and training resources cited below are all freely available online as of this writing. The resources are organized alphabetically by the provider's name, and include a brief description of what each offers on their web site.

Asian Development Bank
The Philippines-based Asian Development Bank has published a compilation of lessons learned in applying futures thinking and Foresight methods with government officials in several developing Asian countries. The publication also defines terminology and offers practical explanations for how to apply Foresight methods (accompanied by helpful images). https://www.adb.org/publications/futures-thinking-asia-pacific-policy-makers

European Foresight Platform
This European Commission-supported platform supports the

international sharing of knowledge about Foresight, forecasting and other methods of future studies. It contains a wealth of materials on Foresight, including the ForLearn guide to using Foresight.

http://www.foresight-platform.eu/

European Political Strategy Centre

The European Political Strategy Centre is the European Commission's in-house think tank. Among other activities, it studies Foresight and anticipatory governance. The Centre has published A Strategic Foresight Primer, written by futures scholar Angela Wilkinson. https://cor.europa.eu/Documents/Migrated/Events/EPSC_strategic_foresight_primer.pdf

Federal Foresight Community of Interest

The Federal Foresight Community of Interest is a forum for US federal employees, think tanks, and industry to network, learn, analyze, develop, and communicate foresight methods and best practices to decision-makers and strategic planners. Its website features presentations on Foresight in US government agencies, monthly newsletters, and links to Foresight organizations and reading materials.

https://www.ffcoi.org

The Finnish Innovation Fund Sitra

Sitra is Finland's fund for the future. It acts as a think tank, promoter of experiments and operating models, and a catalyst for cooperation. Sitra has a Future Maker's Toolbox to help users shape the future of their organizations. The toolbox assists in building a vision, and in viewing, interpreting or shaping futures.

https://www.sitra.fi/en/projects/toolbox-for-people-shaping-the-future/#phase-1-trends-and-signals

Future Motions

The Dutch consultancy Future Motions has prepared an Introduction to Strategic Foresight aimed at those interested in the potential of Foresight to help improve strategic capacities and develop long-term strategies. The guide explains the rationale for using Foresight techniques as part of strategy and planning processes and describes some methods for applying Foresight.

https://www.futuremotions.nl/wp-content/uploads/2018/01/FutureMotions_introductiondoc_January2018.pdf

OECD Strategic Foresight Unit

The OECD's Strategic Foresight Unit supports OECD directorates and committees as well as governments and other organizations in preparing for the future. It convenes the Government Foresight Community, an international network of Foresight expertise. The unit has published a 12-page guide explaining how Foresight can add value to policy making, build anticipatory governance, and transform development cooperation. It also provides examples of how Foresight is growing as a discipline.

https://www.oecd.org/strategic-foresight/ourwork/Strategic%20Foresight%20for%20Better%20Policies.pdf

Policy Horizons Canada

Policy Horizons is the Canadian federal government organization that carries out Foresight work and helps other parts of the government develop future-oriented policy and programs that are robust and resilient. Policy Horizons makes available excellent Foresight training modules, learning materials, and informative videos, and selected reports generated by its Foresight activities.

https://horizons.gc.ca/en/resources/

Prescient

Amy Zalman, a New York-based futurist, and Foresight expert and trainer, founded the firm Prescient in 2000. Prescient provides several online resources, including an introductory guide to Foresight. The guide features "five building blocks of Foresight": a futurist mindset, foresight methods, data and evidence, anticipatory leadership, and a strategic narrative (a story linking the past to the future).

https://prescient2050.com/wp-content/uploads/2019/01/Prescient-Guide-Introduction-to-Strategic-Foresight.pdf

Shaping Tomorrow

Shaping Tomorrow is a web-based foresight, strategy and change management portal for corporate innovation and risk management. It was founded by Mike Jackson, who published the Practical Foresight Guide. The 2013 edition of this guide includes sections addressing: strategic leadership, opportunity and risk management, and overcoming obstacles.

https://www.shapingtomorrow.com/files/media-centre/pf-ch01.pdf

Shaping Tomorrow also provides descriptions of methods used in Foresight and other processes aimed at developing strategies for the future.

https://www.shapingtomorrow.com/webtext/46

Glossary

Backcasting. A planning method that begins by defining a desirable future and then works backwards to identify policies and programs that will connect the defined future to the present.

Black Swan Event. An unpredictable and rare event that has the potential to cause severe consequences. While perhaps obvious in hindsight, a black swan event is not something one would typically expect to occur.

Casual Layered Analysis. A technique that identifies four levels of causality and serves to create new futures by creating narratives and systems. The litany is the official description of reality – the problem as it is. The second level comprises social causes, including cultural, economic, historical and political factors that provide a systemic perspective of the issue. The third layer consists of discourse, and is concerned with structure and the worldview that supports and legitimates it. The fourth and deepest layer presents metaphor and myth, unconscious emotive dimensions of the issue.

Cross Impact Analysis. A method used to assess the likelihood of an event or trend and its dependence on the occurrence of other development or impacts.

Delphi Method. A technique used to survey a panel of experts over multiple rounds to arrive at a convergence of opinion. Between the rounds, survey responses are aggregated and shared with the experts.

Driver. A factor which causes a particular phenomenon to

happen. Drivers are building blocks of scenarios.

Environmental (or Horizon) Scanning. A technique used to detect weak signals as indicators of potentially significant changes, for example, discoveries and innovations in science and technology.

Futures Thinking. A multidisciplinary approach used to reflect on major changes that will occur in the coming decades, and to challenge generally accepted opinion and identify the dynamics that are creating the future.

Prediction. A statement about what will (or might) happen in the future, usually based on feeling, experience or knowledge.

Real-time Delphi. An advanced and more efficient form of the Delphi Method through which respondents participate by completing an online survey. Results are updated as responses are recorded.

Scanning Hit. A piece of information (e.g., appearing in a blog, news story, tweet) signaling a potential change.

Strategic Foresight. A structured and systematic way of using ideas about the future to anticipate and better prepare for change. It is about exploring different plausible futures that could arise, and the opportunities and challenges they could present.

Scenario. A plausible story of how a sequence or development of events might play out in the future.

Scenario Exploration System. A board game that was developed by the European Commission's Joint Research Centre. It enables participants to develop a long-term perspective and consider visions and strategies of different stakeholders that include policymakers at different governance levels, business and civil society representatives and the general public.

Systems mapping. An exercise which studies how key variables interact over time and form patterns of behaviors across an interconnected network.

Trend. A prevailing tendency, direction or movement.

VUCO. A period characterized by volatility, uncertainty, complexity and ambiguity.

Weak signal. Incomplete data that may indicate a wild card or emerging trend.

Wild card. A low-probability, high-impact event that might mark a change in direction for a trend or system.

References

Introduction

1. Council on Foreign Relations (October 2020). Independent Task Force Report No. 78. Improving Pandemic Preparedness from COVID-19, 17.
2. Florini, A. and S. Sharma. (June 2020). Reckoning with Systemic Hazards, Finance and Development, volume 57, number 2, 51.
3. Organization for Economic Cooperation and Development (2019) Government Foresight Community Annual Meeting 2019, https://www.oecd.org/strategic-foresight/ourwork/ OECD-GFC-Annual-Meeting-2019-Summary.pdf
4. Royal Dutch Shell PLC (2020), Shell Scenarios, https:// www.shell.com/energy-and-innovation/the-energy-future/ scenarios.html
5. University of Houston College of Technology (2020), 25% of Fortune 500 Practices Foresight, https://www. houstonforesight.org/25-of-fortune-500-practices-foresight/
6. Marcial, E.; E. Schneider; M. Pio; M. Gimene. (July 2020) Cenários Pós-Covid-19: Possíveis impactos sociais e econômicos no Brasil, Faculdade Presbiteriana Mackenzie, Brasilia.
7. Florini, A. and S. Sharma. (June 2020). Reckoning with Systemic Hazards, Finance and Development, volume 57, number 2, 49.

Chapter 1

1. The OECD definition of Strategic Foresight can be found here: https://www.oecd.org/strategic-foresight/
2. Johns Hopkins Center for Health Security, the Nuclear Threat Initiative, and the Economist Intelligence Unit (October 2019) Global Health Security Index, https://www.

ghsindex.org/

3. O'Toole, B. (August 10, 2020) Futurists Mull What Changes Lie Ahead, Pittsburgh Quarterly.

4. Jones, P. (December 2017) The futures of Canadian governance: Foresight competencies for public administration in the digital era, Canadian Public Administration/Administration publique du Canada, volume 60, issue 4, 657–681.

Chapter 2

1. Futurist Herman Kahn, a defense analyst at RAND, is often credited with laying the groundwork for Foresight in the late 1940s when he began describing the possible ways that nuclear weapons technology might be used by US adversaries.

2. Sutherland, W.J.; S. Broad; S.H.M. Butchart; S.J. Clarke; A. Collins; L.V. Dicks; H. Doran; N. Esmail; E. Fleishman; N. Frost; K.J. Gaston; D.W. Gibbons; A.C. Hughes; Z. Jiang; R. Kelman; B. LeAnstey; X. le Roux; F.A. Lickorish; K.A. Monk; D. Mortimer; J.W. Pearce-Higgins; L.S. Peck; N. Pettorelli; J. Pretty; C.L. Seymour; M.D. Spalding; J. Wentworth; and N. Ockendon. (January 2019) A Horizon Scan of Emerging Issues for Global Conservation in 2019, Trends in Ecology and Evolution, volume 34, issue 1, 83–87.

3. Sutherland, W.J.; E. Fleishman; M. Clout; D.W. Gibbons; F.A. Lickorish; L.S. Peck; M.D. Spalding; and N. Ockendon. (February 2019) Ten Years on: A Review of the First Global Conservation Horizon Scan, Trends in Ecology and Evolution, volume 34, issue 2, 148.

4. Cook, J. (September 21, 2015), An introduction to system mapping. https://www.fsg.org/blog/introduction-system-mapping

5. Policy Horizons Canada, Cascade Diagram Exercise (for a Change Driver), https://horizons.gc.ca/en/our-work/

learning-materials/foresight-training-manual-module-5-change-drivers/5/

6. San Francisco Bay Area Planning and Urban Research Association. (August 2018) Four Future Scenarios for the San Francisco Bay Area. San Francisco, SPUR Regional Strategy, 3–7, 31–40.

Chapter 3

1. Asian Development Bank. (2020) Futures Thinking in Asia and the Pacific – Why Foresight Matters for Policymakers, Manila, ADB.
2. National Intelligence Council. (January 2017) Global Trends – Paradox of Progress, Washington, DC, NIC.
3. Agence Française de Développement. (2015) ADF 2025: Development Agencies, Steering Through Future Worlds, Paris, AFD.
4. European Commission (2020) Future of Customs in the EU 2040, https://blogs.ec.europa.eu/eupolicylab/tag/futureofcustoms/
5. European Commission (September 28, 2020) Customs Union: New Action Plan to Further support EU Customs in Their Vital Role of Protecting EU Revenues, Prosperity and Security. Brussels, European Commission.
6. Food and Agriculture Organization. (2014) Horizon Scanning and Foresight: An Overview of Approaches and Possible Applications in Food Safety – Background Paper 2: FAO Warning/Rapid Alert and Horizon Scanning, Food Safety Technical Workshop, Rome, 22–25 October 2013, Rome, FAO.
7. Organization for Economic Cooperation and Development (2020) Towards 2035: Making Migration and Integration Policies Future Ready, Paris, OECD.
8. UNAIDS (2005) AIDS in Africa: Three Scenarios to 2025, Geneva, UNAIDS.

Chapter 4

1. Olivari, S. (August 4, 2020) These 4 Skills can make the World Better after COVID-19, Geneva, World Economic Forum, https://www.weforum.org/agenda/2020/08/the-four-skills-to-make-the-world-better-after-covid-19/

2. Parkash, S.G. and L. Tang. (June 29, 2020) How COVID-19 is Reshaping the World, https://medium.com/@pmo_csf/how-covid-19-is-reshaping-the-world-3a156eba49f0

3. Burrows, M.J. and P. Engelke. (July 7, 2020) What World Post-COVID-19? Three Scenarios. Washington, DC, Atlantic Council.

4. Deloitte and Salesforce. (6 April 2020). The World Remade by COVID-19 – Scenarios for Resilient Leaders. https://www2.deloitte.com/content/dam/Deloitte/global/Documents/About-Deloitte/COVID-19/Thrive-scenarios-for-resilient-leaders.pdf

5. Wade, M. (2020) *Scenario Planning for a Post-COVID-10 World*, Lausanne, IMD.

6. Dumaine, C. and S. Fisher. (2020) The Covid19 Crisis: What's at Stake? Alternative Scenarios and Implications for the U.S. 2020–2023, Cambridge, MA, MIT.

7. Talwar, R. (2 July 2020) Scenarios for a Post-Pandemic World, https://www.maddyness.com/uk/2020/07/02/scenarios-for-a-post-pandemic-world./

8. The Millennium Project (October 2020) Three Futures of the COVID-19 Pandemic in the United States January 1, 2022, The Millennium Project, Washington, DC.

Chapter 5

1. Redondo, I. (24 March 2020) quoted in, "The Office Created by Ivan Redondo to Foresee Catastrophes did not Smell that of Covid-19," Web 24 news.com

2. Barsa, J. (28 October 2020) remarks delivered at the American Enterprise Institute in Washington, DC, https://

www.usaid.gov/news-information/speeches/oct-280-2020-aa-john-barsa-american-enterprise-institute-over-horizon

3. Lum, R.L. (August 2020) Shredding Our Maps: A Period of Historic Transitions Disrupted, https://www.visionforesightstrategy.com/post/shredding-our-maps

Bibliography

Agence Française de Développement. (2015) ADF 2025: Development Agencies, Steering Through Future Worlds, Paris, AFD.

Asian Development Bank. (2020) Futures Thinking in Asia and the Pacific – Why Foresight Matters for Policymakers, Manila, ADB.

Barsa, J. (October 28, 2019). Remarks at American Enterprise Institute on the Over-the-Horizon Strategic Review, https://www.usaid.gov/news-information/speeches/oct-280-2020-aa-john-barsa-american-enterprise-institute-over-horizon

Burrows, M.J. and P. Engelke. (July 7, 2020) What World Post-COVID-19? Three Scenarios, Washington, DC, Atlantic Council.

Cook, J. (September 21, 2015) An Introduction to System Mapping, https://www.fsg.org/blog/introduction-system-mapping

Council on Foreign Relations. (October 2020) Independent Task Force Report No. 78. Improving Pandemic Preparedness from COVID-19, New York, CFR.

Dixon, T.; J. Montgomery; N. Horton-Baker; and L. Farrelly. (December 2018) Using Urban Foresight Techniques in City Visioning: Lessons from the Reading 2050 Vision, Local Economy, volume 33, issue 8, 777–799.

Deloitte and Salesforce. (April 6, 2020) The World Remade by COVID-19 – Scenarios for Resilient Leaders, https://www2.deloitte.com/content/dam/Deloitte/global/Documents/About-Deloitte/COVID-19/Thrive-scenarios-for-resilient-leaders.pdf

Dumaine, C. and S. Fisher. (2020) The Covid19 Crisis: What's at Stake? Alternative Scenarios and Implications for the U.S. 2020–2023, Cambridge, MA, MIT.

European Commission. (September 28, 2020) Customs Union: New Action Plan to Further Support EU Customs in Their Vital Role of Protecting EU Revenues, Prosperity and Security,

Brussels, European Commission.

European Commission (2020) Future of Customs in the EU 2040, https://blogs.ec.europa.eu/eupolicylab/tag/futureofcustoms/

European Commission. (September 2, 2020) 2020 Strategic Foresight Report – Charting the Course Towards a more Resilient Europe, Brussels, European Commission.

Florini, A. and S. Sharma. (June 2020) Reckoning with Systemic Hazards, Finance and Development, volume 57, number 2.

Food and Agriculture Organization. (2014) Horizon Scanning and Foresight: An Overview of Approaches and Possible Applications in Food Safety – Background Paper 2: FAO Warning/Rapid Alert and Horizon Scanning, Food Safety Technical Workshop, Rome, 22–25 October 2013, Rome, FAO.

Foresight for Food (2020) https://www.foresight4food.net/

Foresight Lab (2017) Pakistan State of Future Index: Anticipating 2027, Islamabad, Foresight Lab.

Garrett, L. (1994) The Coming Plague: Newly Emerging Diseases in a World Out of Balance, New York, Farrar, Straus and Giroux.

Ghiran, A.; A. Hakami; L. Bontoux; and F. Scapolo. (2020) The Future of Customs in the EU 2040, Luxembourg, Publications Office of the European Union.

Inayatullah, S., D. List, and A. Hines, https://libarynth.org/futurist_fieldguide/causal_layered_analysis

Johns Hopkins Center for Health Security, the Nuclear Threat Initiative, and the Economist Intelligence Unit (October 2019) Global Health Security Index, https://www.ghsindex.org/

Joint Research Centre (2019) Scenario Exploration System – the Future of Migration in the EU and Beyond, Brussels, European Commission.

Jones, P. (December 2017) The futures of Canadian governance: Foresight competencies for public administration in the digital era, Canadian Public Administration/Administration publique du Canada, volume 60, issue 4, 657–681.

Kewk, J. and S.G. Parkash. (2020) Strategic foresight: How policy-makers can make sense of a turbulent world, https://apolitical. co/en/solution_article/strategic-foresight-making-sense-of-a-turbulent-world?share=copy&uuid=article

Kuosa, T. (February 2010) Futures signals sense-making framework (FSSF): A start-up tool to analyse and categorise weak singals, wild cards, drivers and other types of information, Futures, volume 42, issue 1, 42–48.

Ladislaw, S. and S. Brannen. (May 20, 2020) Forecasting Covid-19's Course, Center for Strategic and International Studies, https://www.csis.org/analysis/forecasting-covid-19s-course

Lipsett, I. (June 20, 2020) Using Casual Layered Analysis for Transformational Change, https://www.iftf.org/future-now/ article-detail/using-causal-layered-analysis-for-transformational-change/

Lum, R.L. (August 2020) Shredding Our Maps: A Period of Historic Transitions Disrupted, https://www.visionforesightstrategy.com/post/shredding-our-maps

Marcial, E.; E. Schneider; M. Pio; M. Gimene. (July 2020) Cenários Pós-Covid-19: Possíveis impactos sociais e econômicos no Brasil, Faculdade Presbiteriana Mackenzie, Brasilia.

Mahaffie, J. (March 9, 2018) Cross Impact Analysis: a Primer, https://foresightculture.com/cross-impact-analysis-a-primer

The Millennium Project (October 2020) Three Futures of the COVID-19 Pandemic in the United States January 1, 2022, The Millennium Project, Washington, DC.

Morrison, J.S. and A. Carroll. (April 1, 2020) Which Covid-19 Future will we Choose? Center for Strategic and International Studies, https://www.csis.org/analysis/which-covid-19-future-will-we-choose

National Intelligence Council (January 2017) Global Trends – Paradox of Progress, Washington, DC, NIC.

Olivari, S. (August 4, 2020) These 4 skills can make the world better after COVID-19, Geneva, World Economic Forum, https://

www.weforum.org/agenda/2020/08/the-four-skills-to-make-the-world-better-after-covid-19/

Organization for Economic Cooperation and Development (2019) Government Foresight Community Annual Meeting 2019, https://www.oecd.org/strategic-foresight/ourwork/OECD-GFC-Annual-Meeting-2019-Summary.pdf

Organization for Economic Cooperation and Development (June 10, 2020) Strategic foresight for the COVID-19 crisis and beyond: Using Futures Thinking to Design Better Public Policies, http://www.oecd.org/coronavirus/policy-responses/strategic-foresight-for-the-covid-19-crisis-and-beyond-using-futures-thinking-to-design-better-public-policies-c3448fa5/#:~:text=Abstract,the%20face%20of%20high%20uncertainty

Organization for Economic Cooperation and Development (2020) Towards 2035: Making Migration and Integration Policies Future Ready, Paris, OECD.

O'Toole, Bill. (August 10, 2020) Futurists Mull What Changes Lie Ahead, Pittsburgh Quarterly, https://pittsburghquarterly.com/articles/futurists-mull-what-changes-lie-ahead/

Parkash, S.G. and L. Tang. (June 29, 2020) How COVID-19 is Reshaping the World, https://pmo-csf.medium.com/how-covid-19-is-reshaping-the-world-3a156eba49f0

Public Service Foresight Network (Government of Canada) (October 20, 2017) Building a Foresight System in Government – Lessons from 11 Countries, https://www.ffcoi.org/wp-content/uploads/2019/03/Building-a-Foresight-System-in-the-Govt-Lessons-from-11-Countries_Oct-2017.pdf

The Red (Team) Analysis Society. Scenarios for the COVID-19 and Post-Covid-19 Worlds – a Bibliography, https://www.redanalysis.org/2020/07/03/scenarios-for-covid-19-and-post-covid-19-worlds-a-bibliography/

San Francisco Bay Area Planning and Urban Research Association (August 2018) Four Future Scenarios for the San Francisco

Bay Area, San Francisco, SPUR Regional Strategy.

Sutherland, W.J.; S. Broad; S.H.M. Butchart; S.J. Clarke; A. Collins; L.V. Dicks; H. Doran; N. Esmail; E. Fleishman; N. Frost; K.J. Gaston; D.W. Gibbons; A.C. Hughes; Z. Jiang; R. Kelman; B. LeAnstey; X. le Roux; F.A. Lickorish; K.A. Monk; D. Mortimer; J.W. Pearce-Higgins; L.S. Peck; N. Pettorelli; J. Pretty; C.L. Seymour.; M.D. Spalding; J. Wentworth; N. Ockendon. (January 2019) A Horizon Scan of Emerging Issues for Global Conservation in 2019, Trends in Ecology and Evolution, volume 34, issue 1, 83–94.

Sutherland, W.J.; E. Fleishman; M. Clout; D.W. Gibbons; F.A. Lickorish; L.S. Peck; M.D. Spalding; and N. Ockendon. (February 2019) Ten Years on: A Review of the First Global Conservation Horizon Scan, Trends in Ecology and Evolution, volume 34, issue 2, 139–153.

Talwar, R. (2 July 2020) Scenarios for a Post-Pandemic World, https://www.maddyness.com/uk/2020/07/02/scenarios-for-a-post-pandemic-world/

UNAIDS (2005) AIDS in Africa: Three Scenarios to 2025, Geneva, UNAIDS.

Voros, P. (2017) The Futures Cone, use and history, https://thevoroscope.com/2017/02/24/the-futures-cone-use-and-history/

Wade, M. (2020) *Scenario Planning for a Post-COVID-10 World*, Lausanne, IMD.

Web 24 News (March 25, 2020) The Office Created by Ivan Redondo to Foresee Catastrophes did not Smell that of Covid-19, https://www.web24.news/u/2020/03/the-office-created-by-ivan-redondo-to-foresee-catastrophes-did-not-smell-that-of-covid-19.html

CHANGEMAKERS
BOOKS

Transform your life, transform *our* world. Changemakers Books publishes books for people who seek to become positive, powerful agents of change. These books inform, inspire, and provide practical wisdom and skills to empower us to write the next chapter of humanity's future.

www.changemakers-books.com

The *Resilience* Series

The Resilience Series is a collaborative effort by the authors of Changemakers Books in response to the 2020 coronavirus pandemic. Each concise volume offers expert advice and practical exercises for mastering specific skills and abilities. Our intention is that by strengthening your resilience, you can better survive and even thrive in a time of crisis.
www.resilience-books.com

Adapt and Plan for the New Abnormal – in the COVID-19 Coronavirus Pandemic
Gleb Tsipursky

Aging with Vision, Hope and Courage in a Time of Crisis
John C. Robinson

Connecting with Nature in a Time of Crisis
Melanie Choukas-Bradley

Going Within in a Time of Crisis
P. T. Mistlberger

Grow Stronger in a Time of Crisis
Linda Ferguson

Handling Anxiety in a Time of Crisis
George Hoffman

Navigating Loss in a Time of Crisis
Jules De Vitto

The Life-Saving Skill of Story
Michelle Auerbach

**Virtual Teams – Holding the Center When You Can't Meet
Face-to-Face**
Carlos Valdes-Dapena

Virtually Speaking – Communicating at a Distance
Tim Ward and Teresa Erickson

Current Bestsellers from Changemakers Books

Pro Truth
A Practical Plan for Putting Truth Back into Politics
Gleb Tsipursky and Tim Ward
How can we turn back the tide of post-truth politics, fake
news, and misinformation that is damaging our democracy?
In the lead up to the 2020 US Presidential Election, Pro Truth
provides the answers.

An Antidote to Violence
Evaluating the Evidence
Barry Spivack and Patricia Anne Saunders
It's widely accepted that Transcendental Meditation can create
peace for the individual, but can it create peace in society as a
whole? And if it can, what could possibly be the mechanism?

Finding Solace at Theodore Roosevelt Island
Melanie Choukas-Bradley
A woman seeks solace on an urban island paradise in
Washington D.C. through 2016–17, and the shock of the Trump
election.

the bottom
a theopoetic of the streets
Charles Lattimore Howard
An exploration of homelessness fusing theology, jazz-verse and
intimate storytelling into a challenging, raw and beautiful tale.

The Soul of Activism
A Spirituality for Social Change
Shmuly Yanklowitz
A unique examination of the power of interfaith spirituality to
fuel the fires of progressive activism.

Future Consciousness
The Path to Purposeful Evolution
Thomas Lombardo
An empowering evolutionary vision of wisdom and the human mind to guide us in creating a positive future.

Preparing for a World that Doesn't Exist – Yet
Rick Smyre and Neil Richardson
This book is about an emerging Second Enlightenment and the capacities you will need to achieve success in this new, fast-evolving world.